商务英语口语实战丛书

国际商务英语口语

Spoken English for International Business

（修订本）

主　编　张礼贵　廖国强　李咏梅
副主编　陈巧巧　陈沿西　谢丽萍

清华大学出版社
北京交通大学出版社
·北京·

内容简介

本书共9个单元，主要内容包括商务谈判，商务合同签订，订单、订货及退货，商务单证，货物包装，货物装运，货物检验、检疫及验收，期货贸易及汇率，申诉、索赔及仲裁等涉外商务活动。

本书适用于高等院校商务英语及相关专业的学生，同时也适用于国际商务活动的从业者和爱好者。

本书封面贴有清华大学出版社防伪标签，无标签者不得销售。
版权所有，侵权必究。侵权举报电话：010-62782989 13501256678 13801310933

图书在版编目（CIP）数据

国际商务英语口语：高级 / 张礼贵，廖国强，李咏梅主编. — 修订本. — 北京：北京交通大学出版社：清华大学出版社，2019.1（2024.10 修订）
ISBN 978-7-5121-1797-6

Ⅰ. ①国… Ⅱ. ①张… ②廖… ③李… Ⅲ. ①国际商务-英语-口语 Ⅳ. ① H319.9

中国版本图书馆 CIP 数据核字（2014）第 018720 号

国际商务英语口语（高级）
GUOJI SHANGWU YINGYU KOUYU（GAOJI）

责任编辑：	张利军
出版发行：	清 华 大 学 出 版 社　邮编：100084　电话：010-62776969
	北京交通大学出版社　邮编：100044　电话：010-51686414
印 刷 者：	北京鑫海金澳胶印有限公司
经　　销：	全国新华书店
开　　本：	185 mm×243 mm　印张：9.75　字数：292 千字
版 印 次：	2024 年 10 月第 1 版第 1 次修订　2024 年 10 月第 3 次印刷
定　　价：	38.00 元

本书如有质量问题，请向北京交通大学出版社质监组反映。对您的意见和批评，我们表示欢迎和感谢。
投诉电话：010-51686043，51686008；传真：010-62225406；E-mail：press@bjtu.edu.cn。

前言 PREFACE

加入世界贸易组织,标志着我国对外开放新的全方位的推进。在经济全球化的新形势下,中国与世界各国的商务交流与合作也会更加频繁。作为一门通用的国际性语言,英语在国际商务交流中起着极其重要的作用。从事涉外商务工作的人员需要掌握好英语,特别是英语口语,才能更好地开展商务活动。

《国际商务英语口语》正是基于这样的背景而为从事对外经贸工作和其他涉外工作的人员及相关学习者编写的商务英语口语读本,既可以作为高等院校商务英语及相关专业学生的口语教材,又可以作为一种工具书,供相关的学习者参考模仿之用。

《国际商务英语口语》共3册,分为初级、中级和高级,主要内容涵盖了对外商务往来中最为常见的经典对话场景,基本上由易到难渐进地涉及了涉外贸易中所有主要的商务活动。

《国际商务英语口语》在选材上覆盖面广,代表性和针对性强,并且兼具实用性和生动性。在实用性方面,书中所选取的材料均为商务活动中最常见的场景,具有很强的实践性和可操作性,能够有效地帮助学习者进行针对性极强的训练并学以致用,符合应用型人才培养的要求。在生动性方面,书中所选取的材料具有较强的趣味性,易学易懂,能够充分地调动起不同层次学习者的学习兴趣。

《国际商务英语口语》在体系的编排上科学合理。

每单元的开始部分均提供了与本单元话题相关的文化背景，以帮助学习者对此话题有一个更加准确的把握。每单元的主体是日常商务对话的经典范例及常用词汇、句型，学习者可以此为模板学习并熟练掌握其中的一些对话技巧。每单元还就对话中出现的语言难点及重要的国际商务知识给出了详尽的注释，以帮助学习者更深入地理解本单元的主题。每单元的课后练习也紧紧围绕本单元的话题展开，主要有"根据中文提示补全对话"和"根据提供的对话背景模仿特定人物进行情景对话"两大类实操性训练。

为了让学习者能够在涉外商务活动中有效地进行交流，每单元后还附有本单元对话的译文，以供学习者参阅。为了让学习者能够更好地掌握相关话题的对话技巧，每单元最后均提供了与之相关的扩展阅读材料，并留有让学习者参与讨论的问题。

本书为《国际商务英语口语》的高级本，共9个单元，主要内容涵盖商务谈判，商务合同签订，订单、订货及退货，商务单证，货物包装，货物装运，货物检验、检疫及验收，期货贸易及汇率，申诉、索赔及仲裁等涉外商务活动。

本书以二维码的形式动态地向读者提供相关的教学资源，读者可先扫描封底上的防盗码获得资源读取权限，然后再根据自身的学习需求，通过扫描每单元开始处的二维码，获取并使用相关的教学资源。例如，本书中所有的对话均配有地道的MP3录音，学习者扫描二维码后即可收听，并可对照本书的教学材料进行对话模仿训练。

本书在编写过程中参考了大量的文献资料，在此向这些文献资料的作者表示衷心的感谢。编者也殷切地希望本书能够对相关读者的商务英语学习有所帮助。然而，鉴于编者水平有限，书中难免有错漏之处，恳请广大读者批评指正。

编者
2024年10月

Unit 1	Business Negotiation	
	商务谈判 ·································	1
Unit 2	Business Contract Signing	
	商务合同签订 ·····························	15
Unit 3	Order, Order Goods and Return Goods	
	订单、订货及退货 ·························	29
Unit 4	Business Documents	
	商务单证 ·································	41
Unit 5	Packing of Goods	
	货物包装 ·································	55
Unit 6	Shipment of Goods	
	货物装运 ·································	69
Unit 7	Inspection, Quarantine and Checking of Goods	
	货物检验、检疫及验收 ·····················	83
Unit 8	Futures Trade and Exchange Rate	
	期货贸易及汇率 ···························	99
Unit 9	Appeal, Claim and Arbitration	
	申诉、索赔及仲裁 ·························	119
Appendix A	**Glossary**	
	词汇表 ···································	135
References		
参考文献 ···		149

Unit

1

Business Negotiation
商务谈判

Learning Resources

Warming-up

Negotiation is a discussion between two or more disputants who are trying to work out a solution to their problem. This interpersonal or intergroup process can occur at a personal level, as well as at a corporate or international (diplomatic) level. Negotiations typically take place because the parties wish to create something new that neither could do on his or her own, or to resolve a problem or dispute between them. The parties acknowledge that there is some conflict of interest between them and think they can use some form of influence to get a better deal, rather than simply take what the other side will voluntarily give them. They prefer to search for agreement rather than fight openly, give in, or break off contact.

There are different styles of negotiation, depending on circumstances. Where you do not expect to deal with people ever again, and you do not need their good will, it may be appropriate to play hardball. Here you may seek to win a negotiation, while the other person loses out. Many people go through this when they buy or sell a house, which is why house buying can be such a confrontational and unpleasant experience.

Similarly, where there is a great deal at stake in a negotiation (for example, in large scale negotiations), then it may be appropriate to prepare in detail, and use gamesmanship to gain advantage.

These approaches are usually wrong for resolving disputes within a team. If one person plays hardball, then this puts the other person at a disadvantage. Similarly, using tricks and manipulation during a negotiation can severely undermine trust and damage subsequent teamwork. While a manipulative person may not get caught if negotiation is infrequent. This is not the case when people work together on a day-by-day basis. Honesty and openness are best policies in team-based negotiation.

The best approach for negotiation within a team is to adopt a win-win approach, i.e., one in which both parties feel positive about the situation when the negotiation is concluded. This helps to maintain a positive working relationship afterwards.

This governs the style of the negotiation. Histrionics and displays of emotion

Unit 1 Business Negotiation

are clearly inappropriate because they undermine the rational basis of the negotiation and bring a manipulative aspect to it.

Despite this, emotion can be an important subject of discussion. For a team to function effectively, the emotional needs of team members must be fairly met. If emotion is not discussed where needed, the agreement reached can be unsatisfactory and temporary. Be as detached as possible when discussing your emotions. Perhaps it would be best to discuss your emotions as if they belonged to someone else.

Dialogue 1 Wishing to Establish Business Relations

Mr. Kinch (K) and Ms. Zhang (Z) are discussing the possibility of establishing business relations.

K: Hello! I'm David Kinch from America.

Z: How do you do, Mr. Kinch. My name's Zhang Min.

K: Glad to meet you, Ms. Zhang. Before my trip to China, we've sent you a letter seeking for a cooperation. After knowing you'll hold the commodities fair in Changsha, I've decided to come here in person to explore the possibility of establishing business relations with you.

Z: We'd be very pleased to enter into business relations with your firm.

K: Thank you, Ms. Zhang. We learned from your Commercial Counselor's Office in your country that you're one of the leading importers of electronic products in China. We've been in this line for more than twenty years. Here is a copy of our catalogue. I hope some of our products will be of interest to you.

Z: I hope so, too. There is an increasing demand for electronic products, especially computers in China. So, if your prices are competitive, we can come to terms.

K: We think our prices compare favorably with prices of the same kind of products on the world market.

Z: That's good. Well, firstly, we would like to see your exhibits, then study your catalogue and decide what items we are interested in.

K: Sure! On display are most of our electronic products.

Z: I find some of the exhibits fine in quality and beautiful in design. The exhibition has successfully introduced to us what your company deals in. I feel we can do a lot of business in this line. We wish to establish business relations with you.

K: Your desire coincides with ours.

Z: Establishing business relations between us will benefit both of us. It would no doubt bring about closer ties between us. May our friendship last forever!

Dialogue 2 Conditions as a Sole Agency

Mr. Li (L) is discussing with Ms. Hans (H) the sole agency agreement.

L: I'm allowed to discuss with you the sole agency agreement between our two companies.

H: Do you have any specific proposal?

L: As our sole agent, you shall not handle any other same or similar products, nor re-export our products to other areas.

H: That's necessary restriction. How long will be the duration for this agency agreement?

L: Two years. If you want to extend the agency agreement, you must guarantee to increase the annual turnover by 10%. And the sole agent shall adequately advertise and promote the sales of our products throughout the agreed territory.

H: We'll do that since our profits depend on it. What about the commission?

L: We'll allow you a 7% commission and another 2% for the sales exceeding the quota.

H: Very good. We accept it. When do you expect to sign the agency agreement?

L: The agency agreement has been drawn up for the period of two years.

H: *(After checking through the agreement)* The agency agreement was made out with great care and we have found no loopholes in it. We'll arrange the signing ceremony of this agency agreement.

L: I hope we can see eye to eye about the other terms of the agency then.

H: So do we.

Dialogue 3 Driving a Bargain

A and B are negotiating about price.

A: We've studied your offer on stainless steel plates and found your price is on the high side.

B: But you know well that our products are of top quality.

Unit 1 Business Negotiation

A: Yes, I know, but we simply can not order them at this price.
B: Well, for maintaining our business relations, we would reduce our price by, say, 2%.
A: When I say your price is too high, I don't mean it is merely by 2%.
B: What kind of reduction do you have in your mind then?
A: I think a reduction of 10% would be reasonable.
B: A 10% reduction is not workable. You can't expect us to make such a large reduction.
A: Well, how about 8%?
B: Hum, that sounds attractive. I'll consult my general manager and let you know.
A: All right. Let's meet tomorrow to finalize the price.

Dialogue 4 Negotiation Conclusion

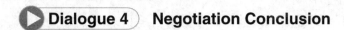

Mr. Zhang (Z) and Mr. Daniel (D) have set up close cooperation.

Z: May I ask how long it takes you to make delivery?
D: As a rule, we deliver our goods within one month after receipt of the covering L/C.
Z: Can you find some way to get round your manufacturers for an earlier delivery?
D: Well, we'll get in touch with our manufacturers and try our best to advance delivery.
Z: When will the goods reach us, then?
D: If there is no accident during transportation, I think the goods will reach you by the end of June. In no case would it be later than July.
Z: Good. We certainly appreciate your close cooperation. I'm glad we've come to an agreement on terms of date and delivery.
D: Our discussion has been very pleasant and fruitful. I sincerely hope that the volume of trade between us will be even greater in the future.

Words and Expressions

the commodities fair 商品交易会
commercial counselor 商务参赞
deal in 经营
no doubt 无疑
authorize *v.* 授权，批准
duration *n.* 持续时间，为期
territory *n.* 代理区域
quota *n.* 配额，限额
draw up 起草
loophole *n.* 漏洞
see eye to eye (with somebody) 与（某人）意见一致

top quality   质量好
business relations   业务关系
workable a. 行得通的
finalize the price   敲定价格

transportation n. 运输
in terms of   在……方面
volume n. 量，数量

1. 商务谈判的特征
（1）以经济利益为谈判目的。

不同的谈判者参加谈判的目的是不同的：外交谈判涉及的是国家利益；政治谈判关心的是政党、团体的根本利益；军事谈判主要是关系敌对双方的安全利益。虽然这些谈判都不可避免地涉及经济利益，但是常常是围绕着某一种基本利益进行的，其重点不一定是经济利益。而商务谈判则十分明确，谈判者以获取经济利益为基本目的，在满足经济利益的前提下才涉及其他非经济利益。在商务谈判过程中，虽然谈判者可以调动和运用各种因素，而各种非经济利益的因素也会影响谈判的结果，但其最终目标仍是经济利益。与其他谈判相比，商务谈判更加重视谈判的经济效益。在商务谈判中，谈判者都比较注意谈判所涉及的产品或技术的成本、效率和效益。所以，人们通常以获取经济效益的好坏来评价一项商务谈判的成功与否。不讲求经济效益的商务谈判就失去了价值和意义。

（2）以经济利益作为谈判的主要评价指标。

商务谈判涉及的因素很多，谈判者的需求和利益表现在众多方面，但价值则几乎是所有商务谈判的核心内容。这是因为在商务谈判中价值的表现形式——价格最直接地反映了谈判双方的利益。谈判双方在其他利益上的得与失，在很多情况下或多或少都可以折算为一定的价格，并通过价格升降而得到体现。需要指出的是，在商务谈判中，谈判双方一方面要以价格为中心，坚持自己的利益，另一方面又不能仅仅局限于价格，应该拓宽思路，设法从其他利益因素上争取应得的利益。因为，与其在价格上与对手争执不休，还不如在其他利益因素上使对方在不知不觉中让步。这是从事商务谈判的人需要注意的。

（3）以价格为谈判的核心。

商务谈判的结果是由双方协商一致的协议或合同来体现的。合同条款实质上反映了各方的权利和义务，合同条款的严密性与准确性是保障谈判获得各种利益的重要前提。

Unit 1 Business Negotiation

有些谈判者在商务谈判中花了很大气力，好不容易为自己获得了较有利的结果，对方为了得到合同，也迫不得已作了许多让步，这时谈判者似乎已经获得了这场谈判的胜利，但如果在拟订合同条款时，掉以轻心，不注意合同条款的完整性、严密性、准确性、合理性和合法性，其结果会被谈判对手在条款措辞或表述技巧上引导掉进陷阱，这不仅会把到手的利益丧失殆尽，而且还要为此付出惨重的代价，这种例子在商务谈判中屡见不鲜。因此，在商务谈判中，谈判者不仅要重视口头上的承诺，更要重视合同条款的准确性和严密性。

2. drive a bargain　讨价还价

Useful Sentences

1. I am interested in your products and hope to induce the cooperation between us.
我对你们的产品很感兴趣，希望与贵公司开展合作业务。
2. We've decided to entrust you with the sole agency for cars.
我们决定委托你作为我们汽车的独家代理。
3. May I know your price terms?
可以知道贵方的价格条款吗？
4. We have cut our price to the limit, we regret being unable to comply with your request for further reduction.
我方价格已降至极限，很遗憾不能满足贵方做进一步降价的要求。
5. Your price is too high to be acceptable.
贵方价格高得令人望而却步。
6. Commission transaction will surely help to push the sale of products.
带佣金贸易肯定有助于产品的推销。
7. Please let me know your lowest possible prices for the relevant goods.
请告知你们有关商品的最低价。
8. It's really impossible for us to make any further concession in your price by allowing you any commission.
对于我们来说，通过给你佣金对价格再做些让步确实不可能。
9. Since the prices of the raw materials have been raised, I am afraid that we have to adjust the prices of our products accordingly.
由于原材料价格上涨，我们不得不对产品的价格做相应的调整。

10. On orders exceeding USD 10,000, we will allow you 5% discount.
    对于超过一万美元的订单，我方将给予贵方5%的折扣。
11. We have already cut down our prices to cost level.
    我们已将价格降到成本费的水平了。
12. Is it possible for you to reduce the price by 5%.
    你们能否把价格降低5%？
13. We usually don't grant any discount for small quantities.
    通常情况下，对于小额订货我们是不给折扣的。

I Complete the following dialogues.

1. **A:** _____.
   （因为我们之间已进行了多年的贸易往来，我方希望贵方此次通融我方。）
   B: Well, we will try our best to satisfy you all the time.

2. **A:** _____.
   （请注意贵方价格与我方现在的市场不相符。）
   B: This is the best we can do. It is very hard to reduce the price further.

3. **A:** _____.
   （我方希望贵方能给予我方 5%的佣金，否则我方将无利可图。）
   B: It seems hard to be acceptable.

4. **A:** _____.
   （让我们各让一半把价格再降 1%。）
   B: It couldn't be better. Thank you for your accommodation.

5. **A:** _____.
   （我们被告知我们的价格偏高。）
   B: Yes, it is so.

6. **A:** How many discounts can you allow us this time?
   B: _____.
   （对于超过五万件的订单，我们经常给予3%的折扣。）

7. **A:** _____.
   （除非贵方提高价格，否则我方将不得不拒绝贵方的订单。）
   B: Well, if it is so, we will cancel our order.

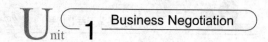

II Situational practice.

The situation: You sell exercise bicycles on behalf of Tianjin Recreation Equipment Imp. & Exp. Co. A businessman from Canada wants to buy 500 sets of your bicycles. Your price is USD 200 per set FOB Tianjin, but he can offer USD 180 per set. You start bargaining.

The task: Create a dialogue about bargaining.

对话汉译

▶ 对话 1 希望建立业务联系

金奇先生（K）与张女士（Z）正在讨论建立业务联系的可能性。

K: 您好！我是来自美国的大卫·金奇。

Z: 您好，金奇先生。我是张敏。

K: 很高兴见到你，张女士。在我来中国之前，我们已给你方来函寻求合作，得知你方将在长沙举行商品交易会时，我就决定亲自来这里，以探讨双方建立业务关系的可能。

Z: 我们很乐意与你方建立业务关系。

K: 谢谢，张女士。我们从贵国的商务参赞处了解到你们是中国电子产品主要进口商之一。我们从事这一行业已二十多年。这是我们的产品目录。我们希望你方会对我们的产品感兴趣。

Z: 我也希望如此。中国对电子产品，尤其是计算机的需求越来越大。因此，如果你方的价格有竞争力，我们有望达成协议。

K: 我认为与世界市场同类产品价格相比，我们的价格很优惠。

Z: 好的，首先我们将参观你们的展品，然后研究你方的产品目录，看看对哪些产品感兴趣。

K: 好的！我们的大部分产品都在那里展出。

Z: 我发现有些产品质量好，设计美观。展览会成功地向我们介绍了贵公司所经营的产品情况。我觉得在这一行业，我们有许多业务可做。我们希望与贵公司建立业务关系。

K: 你们的愿望和我们的愿望是一致的。

Z: 我们之间建立业务关系对双方都有益，这无疑会使我们之间的关系更密切。祝我们的友谊长存！

▶ 对话 2　　商谈独家代理条件

李先生（L）与汉斯女士（H）正在洽谈独家代理协议。

L: 我被授权与贵公司洽谈我们两家公司之间的独家代理协议。
H: 贵公司有什么具体的建议？
L: 作为我公司的独家代理，贵公司不得经营任何其他相同或类似的产品，也不得把我公司的产品复出口到其他地区。
H: 这些限制是必要的。代理协议的期限为多长时间？
L: 2 年。如果贵方想延长代理协议，必须保证使年销售量增加 10%。作为独家代理，贵方应该在整个协议地区进行足够的广告宣传和促销活动。
H: 我公司会做的，因为我公司的盈利取决于此。那么佣金该怎么算？
L: 我公司给贵公司 7%的佣金，对于超过定额的销售，再给 2%佣金。
H: 好极了。我公司接受了。您想何时签订代理协议呢？
L: 我们已拟定好为期 2 年的代理协议书。
H: （阅过协议书后）代理协议书制定得非常仔细，我们没有发现里面有漏洞。我们会安排代理协议的签字仪式。
L: 我希望到那时候我们能在代理协议的其他条款上取得一致意见。
H: 我们也有同样的想法。

▶ 对话 3　　讨价还价

A 和 B 正在对产品的价格进行洽谈。

A: 我们已经研究过你们的关于不锈钢板的报价了。我们发现你们的价格偏高。
B: 但是你非常了解我方产品的质量是上乘的。
A: 我承认，但我们还是不能以这样的价格来下单。
B: 那好吧，为了保持我们的业务关系，我们将价格降低 2%。
A: 我说你们的价格太高了，并不意味着只高 2%。
B: 那么你认为价格应该降低到多少呢？
A: 我认为降低到 10%比较合理。
B: 这是绝对不行的。我们无法那么大幅度地降低价格。
A: 那么 8%怎么样？
B: 嗯，听起来还可以，我得先同我们总经理商量一下，然后告诉你。
A: 好吧，我们明天敲定价格。

Unit 1 Business Negotiation

对话 4   谈判结束

张先生（Z）与丹尼尔先生（D）建立了密切的合作关系。

Z: 请问你们通常要多长时间交货？
D: 我们通常在收到信用证后的一个月内交货。
Z: 你能否设法说服厂家提前一点交货？
D: 那好吧，我们将和厂家联系一下，尽量把交货日期提前。
Z: 货物何时可以抵达我方？
D: 如果运输途中不发生意外，货物估计六月底可抵达贵方。但绝对不会迟于七月。
Z: 好的。谢谢你方的密切合作。很高兴我们在交货日期上达成一致协议。
D: 我们有了一次令人愉快和卓有成效的会谈，我诚挚希望未来我们之间有更大的交易量。

Extended Reading

Preparing for a Successful Negotiation

Depending on the scale of the disagreement, a level of preparation may be appropriate for conducting a successful negotiation. For small disagreement, excessive preparation can be counter-productive because it takes time that is better focused on reaching team goals. It can also be seen as manipulative because just as it strengthens your position, it weakens the other person's.

If a major disagreement needs to be resolved, preparing thoroughly is warranted, and worthwhile. Think through the following points before you start negotiating.

(1) Goals: What do you want to get out of the negotiation? What do you expect the other person to want?

(2) Trading: What do you and the other person have that you can trade? What do you and the other person have that the other might want? What might you each be prepared to give away?

(3) Alternatives: If you don't reach agreement with him or her, what alternatives do you have? Are these good or bad alternatives? How much does it matter if you do not reach agreement? Does failure to reach an agreement cut you out of future opportunities? What

alternatives might other person have?

(4) The relationship: What is the history of the relationship? Could or should this history impact the negotiation? Will there be any hidden issues that may influence the negotiation? How will you handle these?

(5) Expected outcomes: What outcome will people be expecting from this negotiation? What has the outcome been in the past, and what precedents have been set?

(6) The consequences: What are the consequences for you of winning or losing this negotiation? What are the consequences for the other person?

(7) Power: Who has what power in the relationship? Who controls resources? Who stands to lose the most if agreement isn't reached? What power does the other person have to deliver what you hope for?

(8) Possible solutions: Based on all of the considerations, what possible compromises might there be?

(9) Negotiating successfully: The negotiation itself is a careful exploration of your position and the other person's position, with the goal of finding a mutually acceptable compromise that gives you both as much of what you want as possible. Note that the other person may quite often have very different goals from the ones you expect!

In an ideal situation, you will find that the other person wants what you are prepared to give, and that you are prepared to give what the other person wants.

If this is not the case, and one person must give way, then it is fair for this person to try to negotiate some form of compensation for doing so. The scale of this compensation will often depend on the many of the factors we discussed above. Ultimately, both sides should feel comfortable with the final solution if the agreement is to truly be considered a win-win agreement.

The final technique, the formal setting of team rules, comes into play where both assertiveness and negotiation have failed to build good working relationships.

Topic discussion:

1. According to your own understanding, what is the small disagreements in a business negotiation and what is the major ones?

2. If you find yourself in growing a major disagreement with your counterpart, what will you do in order to resolve it?

Unit 1 Business Negotiation

其他常用词汇和短语

Australian dollar 澳大利亚元
Austrian schilling 奥地利先令
average price 平均价格
bargain v. 讨价还价
base price 底价
bedrock price 最低价
Belgian franc 比利时法郎
bottom price 最低价
buying price 买价
Canadian dollar 加拿大元
ceiling price 最高价，顶价
closing price 收盘价
cost level 成本费用水平
cost price 成本价
current price 时价，现价
Danish krone 丹麦克朗
Deutsch mark 德国马克
exceptional price 特价
extra price 附加价
florin（guilder） n. 荷兰盾
French franc 法国法郎
going price 现价
gross price 毛价
Hong Kong dollar 港元
Italian lira 意大利里拉
Japanese yen 日元
market price 市价
maximum price 最高价
minimum price 最低价
moderate price 公平价格
net price 净价

nominal price 名义价格，有价无市的价格（虚价）
Norwegian krone 挪威克朗
old price 旧价
opening price 开市价，开盘价
original price 原价
pound sterling 英镑
present price 现价
prevailing price 现价
price calculation 价格计算
price card 价格目录
price contract 价格合约
price control 价格控制
price current 市价表
price effect 价格效应
price format 价格目录，价格表
price index/price indices 价格指数
price limit 价格限制
price list 价格目录，价格单
price of commodities 物价
price of factory 厂价
price per unit 单价
price ratio 比价
price regulation 价格调整
price structure 价格构成
price support 价格支持
price tag 价格标签，标价条
price terms 价格条款
price theory 价格理论
price catalogue 定价目录
priced a. 已标价的，已定价的

new price 新价	selling price 卖价
pricing cost 定价成本	Singapore dollar 新加坡元
pricing method 定价方法	special price 特价
pricing policy 定价政策	Swedish krona 瑞典克朗
pricing *n.* 定价，标价	Swiss franc 瑞士法郎
retail price 零售价	Unites States dollar 美元
ruling price 目前的价格	wholesale price 批发价

Unit 2

Business Contract Signing
商务合同签订

Learning Resources

Warming-up

A contract is an agreement, enforceable by law, by which two parties mutually promise to buy or sell some particular thing, or to do a certain work. A contract may be formal or informal; it may be oral or written, sealed or unsealed. An executed contract is one that has been fully carried out by both parties; an executory contract is one that is yet to be performed. In an express contract, all the terms are definitely stated whether by oral or written agreement. There is the implied contract, the terms of what are not fully expressed, but are according to the law and fully understood by both parties. The contract which is generally adopted in import and export business is the formal written contract, i.e., a sales contract or a purchase contract; sometimes it is in the form of a purchase order when countersigned by the seller, or a sales confirmation when countersigned by the buyer. The contract can be a business letter after agreement has been reached following an exchange of fax and correspondence. This kind of contract or rather a business letter is, however, seldom resorted to as a formal contract.

Typically, in order to be enforceable, a contract must involve the following elements.

1. Mutual Consent

The parties to the contract have a mutual understanding of what the contract covers. For example, in a contract for the sale of a "mustang", the buyer thinks he will obtain a car and the seller believes he is contracting to sell a horse, there is no meeting of the minds and the contract will likely be held unenforceable.

2. Offer and Acceptance

The contract involves an offer (or more than one offer) to another party, who accepts the offer. For example, in a contract for the sale of a piano, the seller may offer the piano to the buyer for $1,000.00. The buyer's acceptance of that offer is a necessary part of creating a binding contract for the sale of the piano.

3. Mutual Consideration

In order to be valid, the parties to a contract must exchange something of

Unit 2 Business Contract Signing

value. In the case of the sale of a piano, the buyer receives something of value in the form of the piano, and the seller receives money.

4. Performance or Delivery

In order to be enforceable, the action contemplated by the contract must be completed. In a typical "breach of contract" action, the party alleging the breach will recite that it performed all of its duties under the contract, whereas the other party failed to perform its duties or obligations.

5. Good Faith

It is implicit within all contracts that the parties are acting in good faith. For example, if the seller of a "mustang" knows that the buyer thinks he is purchasing a car, but secretly intends to sell the buyer a horse, the seller is not acting in good faith and the contract will not be enforceable.

6. No Violation of the Public Policy

In order to be enforceable, a contract cannot violate "public policy". For example, if the subject matter of a contract is illegal, you cannot enforce the contract. A contract for the sale of illegal drugs, for example, violates public policy and is not enforceable. Please note that public policy can shift.

Dialogues

Dialogue 1 Talking about Signing the Contract

Mr. Bennett (B) and Ms. Zhong (Z) are talking about signing the contract.

B: Good morning, Ms. Zhong. I've come to discuss with you the contract for high technology office equipment. I think I must go into some details face to face with you.

Z: Do you mean that you are prepared to accept our terms? As I told you, our terms are most favorable.

B: Well, it's like this. I telephoned my head office for advice the other day. My boss has agreed to the price you suggested. And I've bought a draft contract with me. Would you like to go over it?

Z: Mm... It's all right for me. Well, I'll agree to sign it.

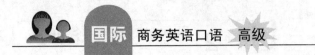

B: Then I'll get the contract typed so that we can sign it this afternoon.

Z: I'm glad we've concluded this first transaction between us. Our next job is to see the contract carried out smoothly. I hope both of us will stick to the terms and conditions in the contract.

B: Sure. A businessman must always abide by the contract, mustn't he?

Dialogue 2   Talking about Terms and Conditions of the Contract

Mr. Fagg (F) and Ms. Han (H) are talking about the details and terms of the contract.

H: Mr. Fagg, if you don't mind, I'd like to go over all the terms and conditions in the contract before signing it.

F: Do it, please.

H: Thank you.

F: Is there anything that's not appropriate?

H: I think there are a few points that need to be clarified in order to avoid misunderstanding.

F: All right. Let's go over the contract clause by clause, shall we?

H: Don't you think this clause should be improved? You see, it's stipulated in the contract that all the goods shall be packed each in a paper box and then in cardboard cartons. It's all right for blouses, but it's not necessary for accessories, is it?

F: No, it's not. Accessories ought to be packed separately.

H: And the contract does not allow partial shipment and transshipment, although they were agreed on during our negotiation.

F: Yes, you are right. It must be clerical mistakes. Let's correct it.

H: Here's another point. Regarding arbitration, we suggested it be carried out in China and the arbitral award be final and binding upon both parties. You know, the Arbitration Commission of CCPIT enjoys a high prestige in the world.

F: OK, I agree.

Dialogue 3   To Add One Provision

Before signing the contract, A and B read through the contract together for a final check.

A: I think there is one more provision which should be added to the contract.

B: Yes?

Unit 2 Business Contract Signing

A: We forget the "force majeure". In the international practice, if the production and delivery are affected by a "force majeure", we are not responsible.
B: That is fair. But it must be stipulated at the same time that you are responsible to notify us the accident within 15 days with the enclosure of the accident certificate issued by relative organization.
A: Sure.
B: And if the "force majeure" lasts over two months, we are entitled to cancel the contract.
A: I hope everything will go smoothly.
B: That's also our wish. If there is no other question about the contract, I will get the contract revised right now so that we can sign it today.

Dialogue 4 Signing the Contract

Finally A and B sign the contract successfully.

A: Now our secretary has the sales contract typed out. Will you take a last look before you sign?
B: With pleasure. *(Examining the contract)* Everything is perfect. Things that should be there are there. You've done a good job.
A: Well then, let's sign it, shall we?
B: Oh, yes, of course. I've been looking forward to this moment.
A: After you. Please sign your name here, here, and here. I'll sign it here, here and here. OK now, each of us has two formal copies of the contract, one in Chinese and one in English.
B: I'm so glad that we have made this deal together.
A: Congratulations on our successful conclusion of business!

Words and Expressions

go over 浏览	clerical *a.* 记录的
carry out 执行	arbitration *n.* 仲裁
stick to 坚持	prestige *n.* 声誉
abide by 遵守	provision *n.* 条款
clarify *v.* 讲清楚，澄清	force majeure 不可抗力
clause by clause 一条一条	be entitled to 有权做……
accessory *n.* 附件，配饰	look forward to 盼望

Notes

1. 贸易合同

贸易合同是一份具有法律效力的协议书。它可以是书面的，也可以是口头的。但在国际贸易活动中所采用的贸易合同绝大部分都是正式的书面合同。

国际货物买卖合同是指营业地在不同国家境内的当事人之间关于一方提供出口货物、收取货款，另一方接受货物、支付货款的书面约定。它是国际货物买卖法律制度的主要内容，也是国际贸易合同中的一个最主要的形式。我国对外经济合同涉及面很广，但货物买卖合同是最基本、最主要的合同，是一份需要卖方签字的购货订单或需要买方会签的销售确认书。

一份正式的贸易合同通常由三部分构成：约首、约文和约尾。

2. standard contract　标准合同
3. draft agreement　草约
4. sole agency contract　独家代理合同
5. model contract　格式合同，示范合同
6. contract law　合同法
7. contractual practice　合同惯例
8. contract value　合同金额
9. termination of contract　合同期满
10. contract period　合同期限
11. contractual obligation　合同义务

Useful Sentences

1. A business contract is an agreement concluded between the sellers and the buyers, enforceable by the law.
   商业合同是买卖双方达成的具有法律效力的协议。

2. We are in agreement on all points. So all that's left is to draw up a contract and get signatures.
   我们已经在所有问题上达成了一致。因此剩下来的事情就是拟定合同和签署合同了。

3. We've come to an agreement on all terms and conditions of the contract.

Unit 2 Business Contract Signing

我们双方对合同的条款取得了一致的意见。

4. As far as the contract stipulations are concerned, there's nothing more. But there are a few minor points which I'd like to have your cooperation.

   就合同条款而言，没什么了。不过有几处小问题，想得到你的帮助。

5. The contract is valid for three years.

   合同有效期为三年。

6. Each of us keeps one original and two copies.

   我们每个人保留一份正本和两份副本。

7. In case one party fails to carry out the contract, the other party is entitled to cancel the contract.

   如果一方不执行合同，另一方有权撤销合同。

8. The contract will be renewed annually.

   合同每年续订一次。

9. You must state the description of the goods, the quantity and the unit price in each contract.

   你们在每笔合同中都必须提到商品的性能说明、数量和单价。

10. The details of the contract can be changed only when both parties agree to the change.

    合同细节只有在双方同意的情况下才能加以修改。

11. The contract can be cancelled upon mutual agreement.

    在合同双方都同意的情况下可以废除合同。

12. Both parties shall abide by the contract and maintain commercial integrity. All breach of the contract will bring about disputes and claims.

    合同双方应重合同守信用，任何违约都会引起分歧和索赔要求。

13. If there is a changing situation at one end and the work cannot be completed at the time originally stipulated in the contract, they have to request the other party to amend relative contract terms.

    如果合同一方形势发生变化，工作无法如期按合同规定来完成，应要求另一方修改合同的有关条款。

Exercises

I **Complete the following dialogues.**

1. **A:** I'm glad that we have come to terms.
   B: _____

_____
（我们感谢贵方的友好合作。希望这笔交易将成为今后其他交易的先驱。）

2. **A:** This copy is for you.

   B: _____
   _____
   （谢谢。我会好好保存它的。可以说，本合同是我们业务关系的开端。）

3. **A:** _____
   _____
   （我想一切都弄清楚了。希望能很快签订合同。）

   B: Thank you. We'll contact you as soon as the formal contract is ready.

4. **A:** Please sign it here, here and here.

   B: _____
   _____!
   （我们终于成功签了合同。请允许我为我们的生意和未来的合作举杯祝贺，干杯！）

5. **A:** _____.
   （请允许我将谈妥的要点再重复一遍。）

   B: OK.

6. **A:** _____
   _____
   （在我们签订合同之前，让我们再把合同要点过目一下。）

   B: All right.

7. **A:** _____
   _____
   （我们每人拿一份正本和两份副本。）

   B: OK.

8. **A:** _____
   （安德逊先生，我们会保证你们的货物将在11月中旬装船。）

   B: Thanks, we will get that in the contract, of course, up till now, I find we have a very happy cooperation.

9. **A:** Glad to hear it. Let's call it a day and go on our talk tomorrow morning, say, at nine?

   B: _____.
   （行，明天九点见，我会按时到。）

10. **A:** If everything goes on smoothly we can renew our contract when it expires.

    B: _____
    （我们也希望如此。）

Unit 2 Business Contract Signing

II Situational practice.

The situation: Through many times of negotiation, the transaction between the IBM corp. and your corp. has been brought to a successful conclusion. Now, Mr. Brown, the general manager of the IBM corp., and you are going to sign a sales contract.

The task: Create a dialogue according to the situation.

对话汉译

对话 1 商谈合同签订事宜

班奈特先生（B）与钟女士（Z）正在商谈合同的签订。

B: 早晨好，钟女士，我是来和您商谈签订高科技办公设备合同的。我想我必须当面和您详细地谈一谈。

Z: 您的意思是打算接受我们的条款了？我对您说过，我们的条款是最优惠的。

B: 哦，是这样的。那天我电话请示了总公司，老板同意您提出的价格。我把合同草稿带来了。请您过目。

Z: 嗯……我看行。好，我可以同意签字。

B: 那我把合同打出来，下午签字。

Z: 很高兴我们达成了第一笔交易。下一步就是保证合同顺利执行了。希望我们双方都能遵守合同条款。

B: 那当然了。商人就应该永远遵守合同，不是吗？

对话 2 商谈合同条款和条件

费格先生（F）与韩女士（H）正在商谈合同的细节与条款。

H: 费格先生，您要是不介意，我想先看看合同条款再签字。

F: 请便。

H: 谢谢。

F: 有什么不当之处吗？

H: 我认为有几点需要写明白，以免产生误解。

F: 好，我们逐一看一看好吗？

H: 您看这一条是否要改动一下呢?合同里写的是所有货物都必须以纸盒包装,外面再用纸板箱包装。就服装而言那没问题。但是对于配饰就没有必要了吧?

F: 不错。配饰应该另行包装。

H: 此外,合同里写明不允许分批装运和转船。可是我们讨论中一致同意是可以分批和转船的。

F: 是呀,一点也没错。这恐怕是笔误了。改过来吧。

H: 还有一点关于仲裁的问题。我们建议仲裁在中国进行。仲裁裁决为终局裁定且对双方都有约束力。你知道,中国国际贸易促进委员会仲裁委员会在世界上享有很高的声望。

F: 好吧,就按您的意思办。

▶ 对话 3　增加合同条款

在签订合同之前,A 和 B 一起通读合同,做最后的检查。

A: 我想还有一个条款应该加入合同。

B: 是什么?

A: 我们忘记"不可抗力"了。根据国际惯例,如果生产和交货受到"不可抗力"的影响,我们将不负责任。

B: 这很公平。但同时必须注明你方有责任在事故发生的 15 天内告知我方并寄送由有关机构发放的事故证明。

A: 当然。

B: 如果"不可抗力"持续两个月以上,我们有权取消合同。

A: 我希望所有的事情都能进展顺利。

B: 这也是我们的愿望。如果关于合同没有其他问题的话,我现在就修订合同以便我们今天就能签合同。

▶ 对话 4　签订合同

最终 A 和 B 成功签订合同。

A: 我们的秘书已经将销售合同打印出来了。请你再看一遍,然后签字好吗?

B: 好的。*(仔细看合同)* 不错,该有的都有了。你们做得很不错。

A: 那么,我们就签字吧,怎么样?

B: 那当然了。我一直在期待这一刻呢。

A: 你先请。在这儿签,这儿,还有这儿。我在这儿签,这儿,还有这儿。现在我们每

Unit 2 Business Contract Signing

人两份正式合同：一份中文，一份英文。
B: 真高兴我们终于做成了这笔生意。
A: 祝贺我们圆满达成交易。

Extended Reading

Signing a Contract Is Not the End

The final important point about negotiation in the business world is the law of contract. It is generally enforceable in the courts. The position is more complicated in international business negotiations because of differences in law and assumed liabilities. But, the courts are a source for remedies if contracts are broken. Suing defaulting contractors is quite common. A sound knowledge of contract law is therefore essential for negotiators drawing up an agreement at the end of a deal.

After a transaction is concluded, a contract is signed by the buyer and the seller. The contract should specify the name of commodity, specifications, quantity, unit price, total value, port of loading and destination, time of delivery, payment terms and sometimes other general conditions of sales. All the terms and conditions in the contract should be carried out in all seriousness. Non-performance of contract may cause disputes and claims. Therefore, it is very important that we should have the contract made out clearly and correctly, and more important, we should abide by it and keep good faith.

However, signing a contract is not the end of a round of, or many-a-round, negotiation but a step in negotiation. A sophisticated negotiator can often take the chance to get more. A negotiator should be aware of the following traps set by the counterpart.

♦ **Chipping away**

Some people will seek a constant stream of small concessions on a wide range of issues, continuing in parallel with the main negotiation on more substantive issues, so they will keep the negotiations open for as long as possible by means of delaying final signature and possibly even continuing thereafter. This can be extremely irritating. They never quite push you too far in one go.

Use threats or an ultimatum to cut the chipping away if you are in a position of strength. No matter in what position, confront the other side despite the risk of negotiations breaking down.

♦ **Dragging into a very complex deal**

As the more complex a deal is, the harder to deal with, some people may like to drag the deal into a complex one and this is an easy job. The complex deals make the other side feel hard to follow and trying to trace the interconnections of the various issues is certainly to become a nightmare.

The old KISS adage (Keep It Simple, Stupid) is useful for all of us. Be sure that you know where your points are, then stand fast there and don't obscure the fact of a fundamental difference.

Topic discussion:

1. When can a contract draft be drawn?
2. Why is it important to go through the contract again before signing it?

其他常用词汇和短语

abide by the contract 遵守合同	come into effect 生效
alter the contract 修改合同	completion of contract 完成合同
annul the contract 废除合同	contract for future delivery 期货合同
approve the contract 审批合同	contract for goods 订货合同
be laid down in the contract 在合同中列明	contract for purchase 采购合同
	contract for service 劳务合同
be legally binding 受法律约束	contract law 合同法
be stipulated in the contract 在合同中予以规定	contract life 合同有效期
	contract note 买卖合同（证书）
breach of contract 违反合同	contract of arbitration 仲裁合同
break the contract 毁约	contract of carriage 运输合同
bring the contract into effect 使合同生效	contract of employment 雇佣合同
	contract of engagement 雇佣合同
cancel the contract 撤销合同	contract of insurance 保险合同
cancellation of contract 撤销合同	contract of sale 销售合同
carry out the contract 执行合同	contract parties 合同当事人
cease to be in effect/force 失效	contract period/contract term 合同期限

Unit 2 Business Contract Signing

contract price　合同价格
contract provisions/stipulations　合同规定
contract sales　订约销售
contract terms/contract clauses　合同条款
contract wages　合同工资
contractor　n. 订约人，承包人
contractual claim　按合同索偿
contractual damage　合同引起的损害
contractual dispute　合同上的争议
contractual guarantee　合同规定的担保
contractual income　合同收入
contractual joint venture　合作经营企业，契约式联合经营企业
contractual liability/obligation　合同规定的义务
contractual practice/usage　合同惯例
contractual specifications　合同规定
contractual terms & conditions　合同条款和条件
copies of the contract　合同副本
countersign a contract　会签合同
draft a contract　起草合同
draw up a contract　拟定合同

enter into a contract　订合同
execute/implement/fulfil/perform a contract　执行合同
execution of contract　履行合同
executory contract　尚待执行的合同
expiration of contract　合同期满
get a contract　得到合同
go (enter) into force　生效
honor a contract　重合同，守约
interpretation of contract　合同的解释
land a contract　得到（拥有）合同
long-term contract　长期合同
make a contract　签订合同
nice fat contract　很有利的合同
originals of contract　合同正本
performance of contract　合同的履行
place a contract　订合同
renewal of contract　合同的续订
repeat a contract　重复合同
short-term contract　短期合同
sign a contract　签合同
tear up the contract　撕毁合同
terminate the contract　解除合同
written contract　书面合同

Unit 3

Order, Order Goods and Return Goods
订单、订货及退货

Learning Resources

Warming-up

Order refers to an oral or written request to supply a specified quantity of goods. It may be the result of an offer or a counteroffer with a positive acceptance. It may be given by letter, telegram, telex or fax, or even orally at a meeting. But order letters are a common form of correspondence for obtaining equipment, service and supplies. An order letter/form must include all the necessary details to make it complete, namely:

(1) Name of commodity, model number, size, color, or any other relevant information;

(2) Quantity;

(3) Date and method of shipment;

(4) Price per item;

(5) Packing;

(6) Payment.

When the buyer sends the seller an order for some goods, he also sends him a confirmation of purchase in duplicate to be countersigned, with one copy to be returned for file. When the seller receives an order, he must send a confirmation of sales in duplicate to the buyer to be countersigned with one copy to be returned for file. And, after receiving the seller's confirmation, the buyer opens a letter of credit, whereas the seller gets the goods ready for shipment after he receives the letter of credit.

When a seller receives the "first" order from a new customer, he must write a letter to acknowledge the order. The letter should include the following:

(1) express pleasure at receiving the order;

(2) add a favorable comment on the goods ordered;

(3) include an assurance of prompt and careful attention;

(4) draw attention to other products likely to be of interest;

(5) hope for further orders.

If sellers cannot accept buyers' orders because the goods required are not available or prices and specifications have been changed. In such circumstances, letters rejecting orders must be written with the utmost care and with an eye to goodwill and future business. It is advisable to recommend suitable substitutes, make counteroffers and persuade buyers to accept them.

Unit 3 Order, Order Goods and Return Goods

Dialogues

▶ Dialogue 1   Placing a Trial Order

Mr. Ketts (K) and Mr. Wang (W) are talking about a trial order.

K: How many computers do you want to order?

W: As is stated before, we'll order 1,000 sets at the very most because your prices are still on a high side though you have adjusted. It would not be easy for us to push the sales if we buy it at this price.

K: If you can order more we would like to make a further concession.

W: Order more? I'm afraid this can't be done.

K: If you order 2,000 sets, we are prepared to make a 2% reduction.

W: You mean you'll reduce your price by 2% on the basis of $870 per set?

K: Of course!

W: Well, let me consider. I'll give a reply to you this afternoon.

▶ Dialogue 2   Talking about the Order

A and B are talking about the order.

A: With reference to your fax dated January 14, we are glad to learn that you have interests in our electric fans.

B: Yes, we do think your products are good in quality and reasonable in price. We intend to place an order with you.

A: That is great.

B: How many will you book the order for the goods?

A: Well, there is a great demand for electric fans in our market for it will be very hot some months later. Well, do you have the goods available now?

B: Absolutely, we have a large reserve in stock at present and you should expedite to order because there will be more orders from our customers in the near future.

A: We do wish you could supply us 10,000 pieces at the agreed price, which will be favorable for us to leave some margin of profit.

B: No problem. We will arrange the shipment as soon as possible.

Dialogue 3 Confirming the Order

A and B are negotiating about the order price of the watch.

A: We have looked at your samples and feel interested in your products. What's your offer for us?

B: I think you must have noticed that our products have good quality and our brand name is very competitive. Our offer is $25 each.

A: We have to point out your price is on the high side and it's impossible for us to push any sales at such a price.

B: Well, to get the business done, we plan to make some concessions. But if the quantity is too small, I'm afraid we can't move much. What's the size of your order?

A: 100 pieces.

B: You are kidding. Don't forget you are buying watches, not motorcycles.

A: We have some financial difficulties at the moment of the customers. Substantial orders from us will follow.

B: In that case, let's conclude the transaction at the price of $23 each.

A: It's settled.

Dialogue 4 Talking about Returning Goods

A and B are talking about returning goods.

A: Good morning.

B: Good morning.

A: We feel regretful to tell you the order we have placed should be cancelled as the war broke out yesterday in our country.

B: Really sorry to hear that. It is really bad for we have done some arrangements for shipment.

A: It is impossible for us to sell the goods now and we wish you could understand and prevent more loss. For the loss arisen, we will compensate some to you.

B: We do thank for your accommodation, but we wish you could order the goods after your country is in order.

A: Definitely. You had better send us the loss arisen and we will consider the amount to make the loss up.

Unit 3 Order, Order Goods and Return Goods

B: When will you need it?
A: It should be as soon as possible. Do appreciate your full cooperation.
B: Hope we have a brighter future to our mutual benefit.

Words and Expressions

as is stated before 如前所述	offer *n.* 出价
make a reduction 减价	on the high side （价格）偏高
on the basis of 基于	concession *n.* 让步
place an order with 向……订购	substantial *a.* 充实的，大量的
available *a.* 可得到的	transaction *n.* 交易，买卖
in stock 有存货	settle *v.* 决定
expedite *v.* 加快（进程等）	accommodation *n.* 通融
sample *n.* 样品	make up 补偿

Notes

1. 订单

订单是为了要求具体数量的货物而提出的一种要求。它是在发盘或询盘后发出报价而促成的结果。订单可用信函发送，也可以在谈判时口头提出。

按照商法，买主的订单是对预购货物的出价，在卖主接受以前，不受法律约束。在接受以后，双方就要履行协议，并受法律的约束。

（1）买主的义务：
① 若所供货物符合订单条款，就应接受；
② 按协议条款支付货款；
③ 尽快检验货物（若货物有缺陷而不迅速通知卖主，则应认为货物已被接受）。

（2）卖主的义务：
① 在协议规定的时间内妥善递交所定货物；
② 保证所供货物不存在哪怕买主在订购时无法知道的缺陷；
③ 若所交货物有缺陷，买主可以要求减价，或换货或撤销订单，还可以向卖主要求赔偿由此造成的损失。

2. order 订购，订单

Useful Sentences

1. If the quality of the goods is up to our expectation, we will place further orders in the near future.
   如果货物质量符合我们的期望,我方在不久的将来将进一步订购。

2. We wish the first order could be executed satisfactorily.
   我方希望首次订单能满意执行。

3. You may rest assured that as soon as we are able to accept new orders, we shall give priority or preference to yours.
   你方请放心,一旦我们能够接受新订单,我方将优先考虑你方的订单。

4. Your order has been carried out with great care, and please open the relevant L/C as soon as possible.
   你方订单已认真执行,请尽快开立相关的信用证。

5. If the prices are reasonable, we shall be able to place substantial orders for the new items.
   如果价格合理,我方将能大量订购新的产品。

6. We regret our inability to accept your orders as the market is tending upwards and the cost of the raw materials are advancing a lot these months.
   因市场有上涨的趋势,这几个月原材料成本上升很大,我方很抱歉不能接受你方订单。

7. We have no choice but to decline your order, as it is quite out of line with the prevailing market at our end.
   因你方订单与我地现在的市场非常不相符,我方不得不谢绝你方订单。

8. In compliance with your request, we have fulfilled your order with the least possible delay.
   按照你方要求,我方毫不迟疑地执行你方订单。

9. Our minimum quantity of an order for this product is 200 cartons.
   订购我们这种产品的起订量为200箱。

10. If the goods sell as well as we expect, we shall send further orders in the near future.
    如果货物的销售情况像我们预料的一样好,我们不久将继续订购。

11. I am sorry to say that we must turn down your order as we have full order books at present and cannot give a definite date of delivery.
    很抱歉无法接受贵方订单,因我方目前订单已满,不能给予确定的交货日期。

12. The shirts we manufacture are sold in only one color and by the dozen. We never sell individual garments.
    我们生产的衬衫只有一种颜色且成打出售。我们从来不单件出售。

Unit 3 Order, Order Goods and Return Goods

13. Thank you for your order No. B2384 which we received today. We are now dealing with it and you may expect delivery within the next four weeks.

我方今天收到贵方 B2384 号订单，谢谢。我们正在着手处理此订单。你方可于四周内收到货。

I Complete the following dialogues.

1. **A:** _____.
   （因我们已就有关条款达成一致意见，请尽快向我方下订单。）
   B: Well, we will do our utmost to do it as soon as possible.

2. **A:** _____.
   （你方订单中的价格过低不能接受。）
   B: That is the best we can do and no alternation is considered.

3. **A:** _____.
   （我方将向你方下一万台电视机的试订单。）
   B: Really glad to hear that and please rest assured of the quality of the goods.

4. **A:** _____.
   （质量优等的货物将会吸引我们的客户下订单。）
   B: Well, we do wish so and it will benefit both of us.

5. **A:** _____.
   （因市场疲软，我方不能接受你方订单，希望你方能降低价格。）
   B: It seems impossible as the cost of raw materials has been advancing a lot since last month.

6. **A:** _____.
   （如果你能毫不迟疑地接受我们的订单，我方将不胜感激。）
   B: We will do our utmost to satisfy you.

7. **A:** _____?
   （你方能按既定的价格向我方供货吗？）
   B: No problem.

8. **A:** _____.
   （我们的订单必须执行，并与达成的条款一致。）
   B: It seems difficult as our goods are out of stock these days.

9. **A:** _____.

35

（感谢你方及时确认我们的订单。）

B: It is my pleasure.

II Situational practice.

The situation: You order 6,000 sweaters. Your customer accepts your order, but can't fulfill it within the limited time. He explains and discusses it with you.

The task: Create a dialogue according to the situation.

对话汉译

对话 1 试 订

凯茨先生（K）和王先生（W）正在进行试订。

K： 你打算定多少电脑？
W： 如前所述，最多订 1 000 台，因为尽管你方进行了调整，但价格还是偏高。如果以这种价格买进，我们很难推销的。
K： 如果你能再多订点，我们可以让些步。
W： 多订？我想这恐怕不行。
K： 如果你们订 2 000 台，我们准备减价 2%。
W： 你的意思是在 870 美元每套的基础上减 2%？
K： 当然！
W： 好吧，让我考虑一下，下午给你答复。

对话 2 商谈订单事宜

A 和 B 正在商谈电扇的订单。

A： 根据你方 1 月 14 日的传真，很高兴得知你方对我们的电扇感兴趣。
B： 是的，我们认为你方的电扇质量优等，价格合理。我们有意向你方订购。
A： 那太好了。
B： 你们要订购多少货物？
A： 因天气几个月后会变得很热，我们市场对电风扇有大量的需求。你方现在有现货可

Unit 3 Order, Order Goods and Return Goods

供吗？
B: 绝对有的。现在我方有大量的现货库存。因在不久的将来将会有大量的订单，你方必须加快下订单。
A: 我们希望你方能按商定的价格向我们提供1万台。这样将给我们留有利润空间。
B: 没问题的。我们将尽快安排装运。

对话3 确认订货

A和B双方就手表价格进行谈判。

A: 我们已经看过你们的样品了，对你们的产品很感兴趣。请问你们的产品给我们什么报价？
B: 我想您一定已经注意到我们的产品质量好，品牌也很有竞争力。我们的报价是25美元一块。
A: 不得不指出你们的价格偏高。我们不可能以这样的价格进行销售。
B: 为了做成这笔生意，我们打算做些让步。但是如果订购的数量太少，恐怕我们不能让很多。你们订购多少？
A: 100块。
B: 开玩笑！别忘了你们是在买表，不是在买摩托车。
A: 我们目前财政上有些困难。如果你们的价格有竞争力，产品的质量又能让顾客满意，随后我们会下大量的订单。
B: 这样的话，这笔交易就定价23美元一块吧。
A: 成交。

对话4 商谈退货事宜

A和B双方正在商谈退货事宜。

A: 上午好。
B: 上午好。
A: 因昨天我国爆发了战争，我们很抱歉地通知你方，我们所下的订单将被取消。
B: 听到这个消息很遗憾，因为我们已经安排装运。真是太糟糕了。
A: 现在我们无法销售货物。希望你们能谅解，避免更多的损失。对于已产生的损失，我们将进行部分补偿。
B: 感谢你们的通融。但我们希望贵国一切恢复正常后，再次订购我们的货物。
A: 绝对的。你方最好将损失的情况寄送给我们，我方将考虑补偿损失的数额。

B: 你方什么时候需要？
A: 尽量快点。很感激你方的密切合作。
B: 希望我们互利的前景更加光明。

EXTENDED READING

Sample Order Letter

From: goodboy@yahoo.com (BCD Co., Ltd.)
To: coolsir@hotmail.com (ABC Co., Ltd.)
Date: June 8, 2015
Subject: initial order
Attachment:
Dear Sir or Madam: 　　We'd like to place an initial order with you on the terms and conditions as follows: Articles: Haier Brand Air Conditioner Specifications: HRAP 35 GW Quantity: 2,000 sets Unit Price: US$ 300/set CIF OSAKA, JAPAN Total Amt.: US$ 600,000 Payment: by irrevocable confirmed L/C Shipment: to be shipped within 15 days after receipt of L/C Insurance: by seller Look forward to receiving your confirmation ASAP. 　　　　　　　　　　　　　　　　　　　Yours sincerely, 　　　　　　　　　　　　　　　　　　　Mike 　　　　　　　　　　　　　　　　　　　BCD Co., Ltd.

Topic discussion:

When you place an initial order with your cooperating party, what kind of information should be made clear in your order letter?

Unit 3 Order, Order Goods and Return Goods

其他常用词汇和短语

accept an order　接受订单
back order　尚未执行的订单
cancel an order　撤销订单
confirm an order　确认订单
execute an order　执行订单
firm order　不可撤销的订单

fresh order　新订单
fulfill an order　履行订单
order　*n.*　订单，订购
repeat order　续订订单
trial order　试销订单

Unit 4

Business Documents
商务单证

Learning Resources

Warming-up

The documents and vouchers used in international trade to deal with delivery, transportation, insurance, inspection, settlement, customs declaration and so on. They are important to execute the contract and complete the transaction. They are also the legal document and legal basis for settling of foreign exchange, disputes and claims. There are four kinds in general: commercial documents, financial documents, official documents and other certificates.

Banks play an important role in facilitating international trade. It does so by acting as an intermediary, either to collect payment from the importer (as in documentary collections), or more usually, to issue a guarantee of payment to the exporter provided that the latter meets certain terms and conditions. These terms and conditions are usually laid down in the documentary credit issued by the bank at the instruction of the importer. Compliance with these conditions by the exporter is evidenced by the provision of the relevant documents, which act as proof that the exporter has fulfilled his obligation under the documentary credit. As a result, documents play a pivotal role in contemporary trade documentation.

In international trade, all documents and vouchers must be in accordance with the related sets of internationally accepted rules and definitions. The international rules which have close relation with the documents are: International Commercial TERMS 2000 (INCOTERMS 2000), Uniform Customs and Practice for Documentary Credits, publication 600 (UCP 600) and Uniform Rules for Collections (URC522).

L/C is a conditioned guarantee opened by the bank at the request of the applicant, promising to honor the draft on due presentation of the documents as specified. An L/C can ensure that the seller gets the payment due to him after shipment and the buyer gets the documents for the goods after payment.

Documentary credits are separate transactions from the contract of sale with which they are related. In documentary credits, banks are concerned only with documents, and their decision whether or not to pay, accept or negotiate under a credit depends solely on whether the documents presented conform to

Unit 4 Business Documents

the terms and conditions in the credit. If the wrong documents are presented, the only way for the exporter to obtain payment is to ask the applicant to accept the documents despite the discrepancies or errors (and to instruct the bank accordingly); otherwise the beneficiary loses the protection afforded under a documentary credit.

Dialogues

Dialogue 1 Insisting on Payment by L/C

Mr. West (W) is talking about terms of payment with Miss Liu (L).

W: Good morning, Miss Liu. It's the fifth time of negotiations. What are we going to talk about today?

L: Good morning, Mr. West. We have agreed on prices and orders. Now what about the terms of payment and the date of delivery?

W: Good. What do you think about the terms of payment?

L: I'm here at your disposal.

W: What is your regular practice about the terms of payment?

L: We usually accept payment by irrevocable L/C payable against shipping document.

W: Could you make an exception and accept D/A or D/P?

L: I'm afraid it's out of the question. We have never made any exception so far because payment by L/C is our method of financing trade in such commodities. What is more, letter of credit is the normal terms of payment universally adopted in international business. We must adhere to this customary practice.

W: I have heard China had adopted the open policy, and you would accept different kinds of payments?

L: Right you are. But that depends on the specific circumstance.

W: To meet you half-way, how about 50% by L/C, and the rest by D/A?

L: I'm sorry, Mr. West. I can't promise you even that. To tell you the truth, D/A is impossible. Perhaps after more business together, we could agree to D/P terms. But now we only accept payment by irrevocable letter of credit payable against shipping documents.

W: To tell you frankly, a letter of credit would increase the cost of our import. To open a letter of credit for such a large order as US$8,000,000 with a bank, we have to pay a good sum of deposit, which will tie up our money and bring us a great deal of difficulty.

L: I see. It may be. But for large orders, we must insist on payment by L/C. You know that an irrevocable L/C gives the exporter the additional protection of the banker's guarantee. And what's more, you may consult your bank and see if they will reduce the required deposit to a minimum.

W: But still we have to pay bank charges in connection with the credit. If you would accept D/A or D/P, it would help me greatly. It makes no great difference to you, but it does to me.

L: The bank charge is very little as compared with our favorable supply. That means nothing. As I have told you, we require payment by L/C.

Dialogue 2   Opening an L/C

Mr. Anderson (A), an agent of an import and export company, is calling Bank of China for information on L/C. (C=Clerk)

C: Hello. Can I help you?

A: Hello. This is Anderson. I want to open a letter of credit.

C: Oh, what kind of credit do you want to open?

A: What kinds of letter of credit are there?

C: There are several ways of division. For example, we may divide letters of credit into documentary credit and clean credit according to whether it is attached to shipping documents or not. The former is frequently used in international trade.

A: International trade? OK, from now on, when I mention L/C, I am referring to documentary credit.

C: Certainly. And L/Cs must state whether they are irrevocable or revocable. An irrevocable L/C can not be modified or cancelled within its valid terms unless the concerned parties of the L/C unanimously agree to do so.

A: Oh, I think the irrevocable L/C is more suitable for me. Could you help me to open it?

C: Sure. Will you come over here? I'll open it for you.

A: Thanks. See you later.

C: See you then.

Unit 4 Business Documents

▶ Dialogue 3 Confirming an L/C

After receiving an L/C, Mr. Woodland (W) is confirming it with Miss Li (L).

W: Hello, may I speak to Miss Li?
L: This is Miss Li speaking.
W: This is Woodland. Good afternoon, Miss Li.
L: Good afternoon.
W: I received your L/C No. 3687 yesterday. Is it a revocable or irrevocable L/C?
L: It is irrevocable.
W: But the credit is not signed "irrevocable", and I can not find the drawn clause.
L: Hold on, I will look it up. *(After a while)* Yes, you are right. In accordance with the sales confirmation (S/C), it is an "irrevocable" credit, and we forgot to notify you the drawn clause.
W: I hope you can send us an amendment as soon as possible.
L: Sure, I'll send you the amendment right now.
W: You didn't write in the unit price of the goods.
L: $300 for each.
W: Where is the port of destination?
L: The destination is Shanghai.
W: What is the latest date of arrival of the shipment?
L: The shipment should be there on or before Feb. 2, 2010.
W: Is transshipment allowed?
L: Not allowed.
W: OK, that's all. I hope you make everything clear next time. Good-bye!
L: Thank you for your reminder. Bye!

▶ Dialogue 4 Negotiating about Insurance

A and B are negotiating about insurance.

A: What does "I" cover according to CIF (cost, insurance and freight) terms?
B: It covers "All Risks" and "War Risks" at 110 percent of the invoice value.
A: Well, obviously we needn't have "All Risks" covered.

B: Why not?

A: Because our imports, aluminum sheet, aren't delicate goods and can't be much damaged on the voyage. FPA will be good enough, I should say.

B: Well, "All Risks" and "War Risks" are our usual coverage for insurance. I'm afraid we can't make the exception.

A: Well, what's the rate of insurance by the People's Insurance Company of China?

B: The rate quoted by the People's Insurance Company of China is moderate. Roughly speaking, the difference between CIF and C&F is about 0.3 percent.

A: 0.3 percent. That seems reasonable.

B: The People's Insurance Company of China has a fine reputation for its good credit as well as its reasonable price.

A: Well, since the choice between FPA and All Risks has little effect on the price, I agree to your term of CIF for this transaction as a trial.

Words and Expressions

terms of payment 付款条件	sign *v.* 签字
date of delivery 交货日期	drawn clause 出票条款
irrevocable *a.* 不可撤销的	sales confirmation（S/C） 销售确认书
so far 迄今为止	
specific circumstance 特殊情况	amendment *n.* 改正，修改
divide *v.* 分割，区分	unit price 单价
documentary credit 信用证	transshipment *n.* 转运，转船
be attached to 附加于	CIF (cost, insurance and freight) 到岸价
valid term 有效期	
concerned parties 相关方	

Notes

1. irrevocable L/C 不可撤销的信用证

不可撤销的信用证是买方银行通过卖方银行对卖方发出的保证付款文件。买方银行称为开证行（opening bank），卖方银行称为通知行（advising bank），承付款的银行称为付款行（paying bank），收受款项的商人（卖方）称为受益人（beneficiary）。所谓不可撤销，是指开证行对它所开出的信用证，未经受益人同意，不得撤销和修改。只要受益人履行信用证规定的条件，即使申请开证人（买方）破产，开证行也必须履行付款义务。

在国际贸易中，凡信用证上未注明"Irrevocable"字样，就应视为可撤销信用证（revocable L/C）。"可撤销"是指开证行可以不经受益人同意，也不事先通知受益人，在付款行付款之前，有权随意撤销信用证或修改其内容。这一点务必引起注意。

    2. D/A（Documents against Acceptance） 承兑交单

按照承兑交单的条件，买方承兑汇票后，就可向代收行取货运单据，待汇票到期时再付款。因此，承兑交单只适应远期汇票的托收。这种方式对出口收汇风险很大，使用时要加以注意。

    3. D/P（Document against Payment） 付款交单

按照付款交单的条件，应先由出口商发货取得货运单据，然后开出汇票连同货运单据一起交银行托收，并指示托收银行，只有在进口商（买方）付清货款时，才能交出货运单据。如果买方不付款，就拿不到货运单据，也就无法提出提单所列货物。

Useful Sentences

1. Our usual terms of payment are by an irrevocable L/C to be established in the seller's favor through the Bank of China.

   我方通常的支付方式是通过中国银行开立的、以出口商为受益人的、不可撤销的信用证。

2. Payment shall be made by us after receipt of the shipping documents specified in clause 10 of this contract.

   我方将在接到本合同第10条所规定的货运单据之后付款。

3. We shall open a letter of credit in your favor, to be settled in US dollars.

   我们将立以你方为收益人的信用证，以美元结算。

4. We require payment by L/C to reach us one month prior to the time of shipment.

   我们要求货款以装运日前一个月抵达我方的信用证来支付。

5. We require immediate payment upon presentation of shipping documents.

   我们求贵方在收到货运单据后，即刻支付货款。

6. Payment by irrevocable letter of credit is convenient for us, and we shall draw a 60 d/s bill on your bank.

   不可撤销的信用证的支付方式对我们来说比较方便，所以我们将向你方银行开立见票后60天付款的汇票。

7. We regret to say that we are unable to consider your request for payment under D/A terms.
   我们遗憾地告诉贵方我们无法接受你们用承兑交单的方式来支付货款的要求。

8. Since you are now short of cash, we can arrange for your payment over 2 months without charges of any kind.
   既然你方目前缺少现金，我们可以安排你们两个月以后再付款，而不附加任何费用。

9. We have opened an L/C in your favor through the Bank of China for an amount of $17,000 to cover the full CIF value of our order No. 754.
   我方已通过中国银行开立以贵方为受益人、数额为17 000美元的信用证来支付编号为754订单的所有到岸价的货款。

10. Please insure for us these products at invoice value plus 10% (at 110% of the invoice value).
    请按票面价值加10%为我们投保这些商品。

11. Please hold us covered for the cargo listed on the attached sheet.
    请为我们附页上列出的商品投保。

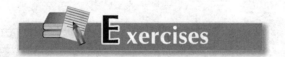

I Complete the following dialogues.

1. **A:** Let's decide on the terms of payment.
   B: _____.
   （好吧，这正是我想要谈的。）

2. **A:** _____.
   （好吧，从长计议，这一次我们接受承兑交单，但下不为例。）
   B: Thank you very much for your application.

3. **A:** Could you think about your terms of payment once again?
   B: _____.
   （恐怕不行，我们采取这种方式是为了与国际惯例保持一致。）

4. **A:** As the peak season is coming, we would like you to deliver by October.
   B: _____.
   （我们保证我们能做到。）

5. **A:** _____.
   （如贵方未能按时付款，我方将终止合同。）
   B: You can rest assured that.

Unit 4 Business Documents

II Situational practice.

The situation: Before A and B are going to visit the Pudong New District, A suggests to pay B by means of D/P or D/A, but B sticks to the payment by L/C. They can't reach an agreement and promise to talk about it the next day.

The task: Create a short dialogue according to the situation.

对话汉译

▶ 对话 1   坚持用信用证付款

韦斯特先生（W）和刘小姐（L）正在商谈付款条件。

W: 早上好，刘小姐。谈判已进行到第五轮了。我们今天谈点什么呢？
L: 早上好，韦斯特先生。我们就价格和订货问题已达成了协议，现在谈谈付款条件和交货日期，怎么样？
W: 好的。关于付款条件，你有什么建议？
L: 我正想听取你的意见。
W: 一般情况下，你们采取什么付款方式？
L: 我们采用不可撤销的、凭装船单据付款的信用证。
W: 你们能否来个例外，接受承兑交单或付款交单。
L: 恐怕不可能。我们迄今为止从未有例外，因为对于这种商品，以信用证支付，是我们进行贸易融资的一种方式。而且，信用证是国际贸易中普遍采用的付款方式，我们必须坚持这种习惯做法。
W: 听说中国实行开放政策，你们接受不同的支付方法，对吧？
L: 是的。不过，那得依具体情况而定。
W: 我们都退一步吧，50%的用信用证，其余的用承兑交单怎么样？
L: 对不起，韦斯特先生，即使那样，我也不能答应你。说实在的，承兑交单不可行。也许以后彼此生意做多了，我们可以同意付款交单条件。但是现在我们只接受不可撤销的凭装船单据付款的信用证。
W: 坦率地对你说，信用证会增加我们的进口成本。在银行开出货价为 800 万美元的信用证，我们得付一大笔押金，这样就会占压我们的资金，给我们带来许多困难。
L: 我知道，那有可能。但是对于大的订单，我们必须坚持用信用证付款。你知道，不可撤销的信用证给出口商增加了银行的担保。再说，你也可以和银行商量，能否把押金减到最低限度。

W：不过，即便这样，我们在开立信用证时，还要付给银行手续费。假使你方能接受承兑交单或付款交单，那就帮了我们的大忙。这对你来说，区别不大，但对我来说，关系可大了。

L：与我们的优惠供货相比，银行的手续费就显得微乎其微了。那就算不了什么。我已经告诉你了，我们要求用信用证付款。

对话2　开立信用证

安德森先生（A）是一名进出口公司的代理，他正在电话询问中国银行开立信用证。（C=银行职员）

C：您好，我能为您做点什么吗？
A：您好，我是安德森，我想开一张信用证。
C：您想开哪一种信用证？
A：都有哪些种类呢？
C：有好几种分类的方法，比如说，根据信用证是否附有装船单据，可分为跟单信用证和光票信用证。前一种在国际贸易中使用较多。
A：国际贸易？好吧，从现在起我所说的信用证是指跟单信用证。
C：好的，所有的信用证必须注明是可撤销信用证还是不可撤销信用证。不可撤销信用证在其有效期内不可修改或撤销，除非相关各方一致同意方可取消。
A：我想不可撤销信用证比较适合我，您能帮我开一张吗？
C：当然可以，请到我行来一趟好吗？我帮您开证。
A：谢谢，一会儿见。
C：再见。

对话3　确认信用证

收到信用证后，伍德兰先生（W）正和李小姐（L）确认信用证。

W：您好，请李小姐接电话，好吗？
L：我就是。
W：我是伍德兰。下午好，李小姐。
L：下午好。
W：我昨天收到你方第3687号信用证，它是可撤销还是不可撤销的信用证？

Unit 4 Business Documents

L： 不可撤销的。

W： 但证上并未注明"不可撤销"字样，而且我方没找到出票条款。

L： 请稍等，我查一下。（过了一会儿）是的，您说对了。根据销售合同，那是一张不可撤销信用证，而我们忘记告知你方出票条款了。

W： 我希望你方尽快将修正后的文件寄给我。

L： 好的，我现在就给你寄。

W： 您没标明货物的单价。

L： 每件300美元。

W： 目的港在哪儿？

L： 目的港是上海。

W： 货船最晚到达是哪一天？

L： 货船会于2010年2月2日当天或之前抵达。

W： 允许转运吗？

L： 不允许。

W： 好了，就这些了。希望你下次要填清楚。再见！

L： 谢谢您的提醒。再见！

▶ 对话 4　商谈保险条款

A 和 B 正在商议保险条款。

A： 在"CIF"中，"I"包括什么？

B： 包括一切险和战争险，按保费发票金额110%投保。

A： 很明显，我们不需要一切险。

B： 为什么？

A： 因为我们的货物——铝板不是易碎品，航行途中不可能损坏太多，保个平安险就可以了。

B： CIF价格条件中保险种类为一切险和战争险是我们通常的做法，恐怕我们这次不能例外。

A： 那么中国人民保险公司的费率是多少呢？

B： 中国人民保险公司所收的费用很少，大体上讲，CIF和C&F之间的差价大约为0.3%。

A： 0.3%，很合理。

B： 中国人民保险公司以其资信可靠和费用合理而著称。

A： 既然平安险与一切险的选择对价格的影响微乎其微，我同意你方的CIF价格条件。

Extended Reading

How a Letter of Credit Works

A business called InCosmetika from time to time imports goods from a business called ACME, which banks with the ABC Bank. InCosmetika holds an account at the Commonwealth Bank. InCosmetika wants to buy $500,000 worth of merchandise from ACME, who agrees to sell the goods and give InCosmetika 60 days to pay for them, on the condition that they are provided with a 90-day letter of credit for the full amount. The steps to get the letter of credit would be as follows:

(1) InCosmetika goes to The Commonwealth Bank and requests a $500,000 letter of credit, with ACME as the beneficiary.

(2) The Commonwealth Bank can issue an letter of credit either on approval of a standard loan underwriting process or by InCosmetika funding it directly with a deposit of $500,000 plus fees which are typically between 1% and 8% of the face value of the letter of credit.

(3) The Commonwealth Bank sends a copy of the letter of credit to the ABC Bank, which notifies ACME that payment is available and they can ship the merchandise InCosmetika has ordered with the full assurance of payment to them.

(4) On presentation of the stipulated documents in the letter of credit and compliance with the terms and conditions of the letter of credit, the Commonwealth Bank transfers the $500,000 to the ABC Bank, which then credits the account of ACME for that amount.

(5) Note that banks deal only with documents required in the letter of credit and not the underlying transaction.

(6) Many exporters have mistakenly assumed that the payment is guaranteed after receiving the letter of credit. The issuing bank is obligated to pay under the letter of credit only when the stipulated documents are presented and the terms and conditions of the letter of credit have been met.

Topic discussion:

Talk with each other about what the difference between payment by L/C and by D/P or D/A is.

Unit 4 Business Documents

 其他常用词汇和短语

acknowledgement of order　订单确认
air waybill　空运单
agreement to pay　支付协议
bank bill　银行汇票
banker's draft　银行汇票
bank money　银行票据，银行货币
bill of exchange　汇票
bill of lading copy　副本提单
blanket order　总订单
booking request　订舱申请
certificate of analysis　分析证书
certificate of conformity　一致性证书
certificate of quality　质量证书
certificate of registry　船舶登记证书
consignment order　寄售单
contract　n. 合同
delivery instructions　交货说明
delivery note　交货通知
delivery release　发货通知
delivery schedule　交货计划表
dispatch order　发运单
dispatch advice　发运通知
empty container bill　空集装箱提单
enquiry list　询价单
exchange control declaration　结汇核销单
export license application　出口许可证申请表
hire order　租用单
insurance certificate　保险凭证
insurance declaration sheet/bordereau　保险申报单/明细表
insurer's invoice　保险人发票
insurance policy　保险单
invoicing data sheet　产品售价单
mate's receipt　大副收据
original bill of lading　正本提单
packing instruction　包装说明
packing list　装箱单
post receipt　邮政收据
price/sales catalogue　价格/销售目录
product performance report　产品性能报告
product specification report　产品规格报告
promissory note　本票
purchase order　订购单
remittance advice　汇款通知
sample order　样品订单
sea waybill　海运单
shipper's letter of instructions (air)　托运人说明书（空运）
shipping instructions　装船指示，装运说明
stores requisition　领料单，库存物资请领单
swap order　换货单
tanker bill of lading　油轮提单
test report　测试报告
weight certificate　重量证书
weight list　重量单

Unit 5

Packing of Goods
货物包装

Learning Resources

Warming-up

Packaging is the science, art and technology of enclosing or protecting products for distribution, storage, sale, and use. Packaging also refers to the process of design, evaluation, and production of packages. Packaging can be described as a coordinated system of preparing goods for transport, warehousing, logistics, sale, and end use. Packaging contains, protects, preserves, transports, informs, and sells.

Packaging has both protective and promotional aspects. In determining whether the same packaging can be used for foreign markets, marketers must consider a variety of marketplace conditions. Packaging must allow the product to reach its destination without damage. Markets with long, slow, or poor distribution channels may require sturdier packaging. Climatic extremes may necessitate packaging modifications.

Dialogues

Dialogue 1 Making out Packaging Scheme

Mr. Chen (C) is talking about packaging scheme with Miss Liu (L).

L: Did you go into the matter of assembling units overseas, Mr. Chen?

C: Yes. We drafted a plan that we'd like you to consider. It's along the lines of the 4-unit scheme that you proposed.

L: Four units? That would be frame wheels, handle-bars, chains and cranks.

C: That's right. The scheme was drawn up and then passed on to our packing department for recommendations as to crating of the units. Here's their layout.

L: I see. Three crates, frames in one, handle-bars in another, wheels, cranks and chainwheels in the other. That should be all right.

C: Here's a table of crate dimensions, net and gross weights of the contents. The number of frames determines the number of the other units in the shipment.

L: Couldn't you put more wheels in a case? That case seems to be on the small side.

Unit 5 Packing of Goods

C: We could make bigger cases and put more wheels in. But as I said, the frames limit the number of the other units. Twelve frames, twelve handle-bars, twenty-four wheels, twelve chainwheels and twenty-four cranks.

L: Yes, of course. You agree to our suggestion that the saddle could be made locally, I suppose.

C: Well, the price you gave is 10 percent below our CIF figure, so we certainly think you should provide the saddles.

L: That price of ours, by the way, is for a minimum quantity of 1,000 saddles.

C: Yes, I noticed that. To what extent would local assembly help sales, did you say?

L: Twenty to thirty percent. But we proposed the plan for the storage and delivery viewpoint. As to say, less warehouse space and prompt-delivery.

C: Yes, of course. Assembly would be quite a simple matter in a very short time.

L: Sales have been exceptionally good during the past twelve months.

C: Yes, I've noticed that. Where have you been placing them?

L: All in the local market. One or two suggestions that came in from the distributors might interest you.

C: Yes. What were they? Anything that will help sales?

L: Perhaps. General opinion is that the rear carrier should be offered as an extra.

C: That's to keep the price down, I suppose. I'll take it up with our overseas department and listen to what they've got to say about this.

L: Thanks.

▶ Dialogue 2   Persuading Somebody to Accept Packing

Miss Liu (L) is trying to persuade Mr. West (W) to accept corrugated cardboard boxes as packing.

W: Miss Liu, I'm very glad that we have agreed on prices, quantity, and the terms of payment and the date of delivery. What shall we talk about this time?

L: The next problem I'd like to bring up for discussion is packing.

W: Well, let's change to another topic — packing. I'd like to hear what you say concerning the matter of packing.

L: I think different articles require different packing. As for textiles, we usually use corrugated cardboard boxes.

W: You are probably right. But if these goods are to be transshipped on the way, don't you think the goods might be spoiled by dampness or rain. We hope that you can make improvement on your packing.

L: Oh, don't worry about it. Every box is lined with waterproof material.

W: I'm afraid that the cardboard boxes are not strong enough for ocean transportation.

L: But I would think corrugated cardboard boxes are good enough for such lightweight articles as textiles. The boxes are comparatively light, and therefore easy to handle. They'll not be stowed away with the heavy cargo. Besides, we'll reinforce the boxes with metal straps.

W: Well, Miss Liu, I'd rather play safe. Cardboard boxes are easier to cut open, and there is the risk of pilferage to be taken into account.

L: On the other hand, tampering with cardboard boxes can be easily detected. That would prevent people from trying their hands on such packing. What's more, our cardboard boxes are made of special materials, light, but strong.

W: But still I'm afraid that in case of damage or pilferage, the insurance company might refuse indemnification on the grounds of improper packing.

L: You needn't worry about it. The cardboard boxes are strong enough for sea voyage and extensively used for such articles in the international trade. The insurance companies have no occasion to refuse indemnification on such grounds.

W: Well, Miss Liu, if you could guarantee that, we'd be quite willing to accept cardboard boxes.

L: Oh, Mr. West, don't you think you'd better take this up with your insurance company? The most we can do is to assure you that the packing will be seaworthy, but we can't commit ourselves to anything beyond that.

Dialogue 3 Dealing with the Labeling Problem

Tom (T) and Chen (C) are negotiating about how to deal with the regulations of Food and Drug Administration (FDA) on the food label.

T: I wish to make it clear at the outset that this matter of label is entirely our problem.

C: I should say it is something we have never come across before.

T: The Federal Food and Drug Administration, or the FDA as we call it for a short, imposes a whole set of regulations on the import of food products to the United States. Over the years, they have become so rigid and complicated that they are now quite a headache for our importers.

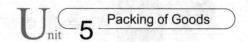

C: In my opinion, overly strict regulations are just another way of restricting imports.

T: Ah, there're something in what you are saying. According to the present FDA regulations, the Ma Ling Labels, as they are, cannot be used if the lichee is to be offered for import into the US.

C: Why not? Our canned lichee and other canned provisions have already been widely sold in various markets abroad, and the Ma Ling Label has now been accepted by most of the overseas customers and importers. Is it quite impossible for you to use the Ma Ling Labels as they are?

T: I'd be quite willing to if I could, but we must comply with the label requirements according to our law, or we can't take the consignments of lichee through the customs.

C: In that case, what can we do to help you? Have you any suggestions?

T: Would you consider quoting us for the order with neutral cans on a CIF basis for delivery in Hong Kong? Our associated company there will have the labels printed to comply with the FDA regulations.

C: Do you think that's the only way out? You know we usually do the labeling ourselves as we are responsible for the brand labels of our products.

T: Well, the present label won't do. Is it possible for you to get round the Ma Ling factory to print different labels for us?

C: Yes, I think they might consider it as long as your requirements are reasonable.

T: This is great. I could wish for nothing better.

Dialogue 4 Packing for Drugs

Ms. Li (L) is introducing the packing of drugs to Mr. Green (G).

G: Ms. Li, how do you do?

L: Mr. Green, how do you do? Welcome to China.

G: Thanks, I'm glad to be here again.

L: Please have a seat. I'm told that you'd like to know something about the packing of the drugs. Is that right?

G: Yes, the main purpose of my visit today is to see the samples of the packing, since it has such a close bearing on sales.

L: True. It also affects the reputation of our products, so we also pay close attention to the packing.

G: Some years ago, we bought some drugs that didn't sell well merely due to the poor packing, so we made a loss on them.

L: Mr. Green, that's something unusual. You need to have a look at the new packing. I think you will find it beautiful and quite well-done.

G: Could you please let me have a look?

L: Yes, here we are in the show room. Take these tablets for instance. They've been packed in plastic bottles and ten bottles into a box. It is easy for the tourist to carry. When drugs are finished, the empty box is still a small piece of art work.

G: Beautiful. Your packing is far beyond my expectation. How about the injections?

L: Most of the injections are put into plastic bottles, and some of them in glass bottles. Ten bottles are put into a box and 200 boxes into a carton. Each case is lined with foam plastics, so the drugs are well-protected against press.

G: Good, very good. What have you done with the Chinese medicine pills?

L: Each pill is put into a small box sealed with wax. Then, ten boxes are placed in a satin-covered rectangular box, lined with beautiful silk ribbon.

G: Excellent. You've improved a lot more than before, but who bears the packing charge?

L: Buyers pay. Practically, packing charge is about 5% of the total cost of the drugs. Normally packing charge is already included in the contract price, and so is this deal.

G: As long as the quality is good and the material is safe during transit, it hardly matters if the price is a little bit higher.

L: You are really one expert in this line. Do you have any more questions or demands regarding packing?

G: No, thanks for what you've shown me. I'm quite clear on everything. Thanks for your very detailed explanation.

Words and Expressions

along the lines of sth./along those lines 同一类的东西
pass on to 传递给……
layout *n.* 布局，安排，设计
net weight 净重
gross weight 总重，毛重
on the small side 较小
corrugated cardboard boxes 瓦楞纸纸箱
to stow away with… 和……放在一起，与……收存在一起
to play safe 注意安全，稳重行事
to take… into account (consideration) 考虑，把……考虑进去

Unit 5 Packing of Goods

prevent sb. from doing sth. 阻止某人做某事	（美国）食品及药物管理局
on the grounds of … 因为……，由于……	quote v. 报价
	associated company 联号，联营公司
Food and Drug Administration (FDA)	have a bearing on 与……有关，对……有影响

1. 常用的有关包装种类的表达有：

outer packing　外包装，即 transport packing　运输包装
inner packing　内包装，即 sales packing　销售包装
neutral packing　中性包装
waterproof packing　防水包装
dampproof packing　防潮包装
shockproof packing　防震包装
seaworthy packing　海运包装
tropical packing　适应热带气候的包装
customary packing　普通包装，习惯包装
cardboard packing　硬纸盒包装
plastic packing　塑料包装
paper packing　纸包装

2. 包装的分类

从包装的作用来看，商品的包装可分为运输包装和销售包装两大类。包装工作涉及包装材料的选用、容器结构和造型的确定、包装方法及装潢设计等各个方面。商品包装是商品在生产和流通过程中保护商品品质完好和数量完整的一种手段。在对外贸易中，做好商品的包装和装潢，还能起到美化商品、提高出口商品竞争能力、扩大销售的作用。进出口商品除散装货和裸装货外、大多数商品都需要包装，它不仅有助于运输、储存和装卸，节约运费，减少破损，而且还便于销售。为了防止货物在运输途中的震动、破碎、受潮或锈蚀等，在包装中通常还使用纸屑、纸条及泡沫塑料等衬垫物。在外包装上一般都印有运输标志，习惯称为唛头。其目的是识别货物，以便运输和装卸。运输标志一般包括 3 个部分。

（1）收货人或发货人的标记以及简单的几何图形。

（2）目的港名称。

（3）件号（件号包括该批货物总件数及该件货物的顺序号，一般要求两者都印刷上）。

此外，根据货物的性质往往要印刷上指示性或警告性标志，以提醒搬运和装卸人员在操作时注意，如"此端向上""保持干燥""易燃品"等。

Useful Sentences

1. This kind of packing costs more.
   这种包装费用很大。
2. A wrapping that catches the eye will certainly help push the sales.
   吸引人的包装当然能够促进销售。
3. Strong packing will ensure the goods against any possible damage during transit.
   坚固的包装可以确保货物在运输中不受损坏。
4. Woolen sweaters will be wrapped in polybags and packed in standard export cartons.
   我们用塑料袋将羊毛衫装好，再装进标准出口纸板箱。
5. Your suggestion on packing is welcome.
   欢迎你对包装提出建议。
6. Your comments on packing have been passed on to our manufacturers for their reference.
   你方对包装的建议已转交我方制造厂商以供参照。
7. We'll contact our manufacturers about the packing.
   有关包装的事情，我们将与生产部门联系。
8. We often present the silk scarf as a gift, so it should be tastefully packed.
   我们常把真丝围巾作为馈赠礼物，因此包装要雅致。
9. The new packing of this article is exquisitely designed.
   这种货物的新包装是精心设计的。
10. The new packing for our tea sets is in Chinese traditional style and we are confident that it will attract the customers.
    我们茶具的新包装具有中式传统风格，我们相信这种包装会吸引顾客。
11. By no means should second-hand cases be used.
    无论如何不能用旧箱子。
12. Taking into consideration the transport conditions at your side, we have especially reinforced our packing.

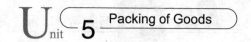

考虑到你方运输条件，我们特别加强了包装。

13. We have reinforced our packing so as to minimize damage which may occur to the goods.
    我方已加固了包装以使货物可能遭受的损失降到最低限度。

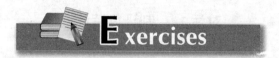

I Complete the following dialogues.

1. **A:** _____?
   （我给你提些建议，你不介意吧？）
   B: No, go ahead.

2. **A:** _____.
   （你们的产品很好，但是你们的包装需要改进。）
   B: Could you be more specific?

3. **A:** A packing that catches the eye will help us push the sales.
   B: _____.
   （我相信新包装一定会使您的客户满意。）

4. **A:** _____.
   （在外包装上请标明"小心轻放"字样。）
   B: Don't worry, we will do it.

5. **A:** Why use wooden cases?
   B: _____.
   （恐怕纸箱不够结实，经受不起装这么重的货物。）

II Situational practice.

The situation: You represent Nanfang Native Produce and Animal By-products Imp. & Exp. Corp. A businessman from Korea has ordered a total of USD10, 000 worth of your bamboo ware. He is not sure what kind of packing would be most appropriate for his orders. You suggest paper cartons according to different sizes of the products.

The task: Now you discuss this issue with him.

对话汉译

对话1　制订包装计划

陈先生（C）正在和刘小姐（L）讨论制订包装计划。

L：陈先生，在海外组装零件之事，你考虑过了没有？

C：考虑过了。根据你所建议的"四零件方案"，我们草拟了一份计划，想请你过目一下。

L：四零件方案？那一定是主车轮、车把、齿链和曲柄吧。

C：正是。这项方案已拟好了，并已送交我方包装部，以便在有关零件装箱方面听听他们的意见。这就是他们的构想。

L：我知道了，是以三个板箱包装。车架装一箱，车把另装一箱，车轮、曲柄、飞轮再装另外一箱。这样应该很好。

C：这是板条箱的尺寸、内装物的净重和总重表。车架的数量决定其他零件的装运数量。

L：你们不能在一个箱子内多装些车轮吗？那箱子似乎小了一点儿！

C：我们可以用大一点儿的箱子多放一些轮子。但是我已经说过，车架限制了其他零件的数量。如果车架放12个的话，其他则放12对车把、24个车轮、12个飞轮和24个曲柄。

L：对呀！那是当然的，我想贵公司同意我方的建议，将车座放在我们国内制造。

C：你们所给的价格低于我们这里CIF价格的10%，所以我方认为理当由贵公司提供车座。

L：对了。我们的价格是最低制造数量在1 000个车座的报价。

C：是的，那个我知道，依你的意思，多大程度上在贵国组装有利于销售呢？

L：20%～30%。但我方建议的计划是以库存和交货为着眼点，换言之，尽量减少库存空间并加快出货。

C：是的，那当然。组装是非常简单的，能在极短的时间内将它们组装起来。

L：在过去的12个月内，销售异常好。

C：是的，这我注意到了。你们将它销售到哪里呢？

L：国内各地市场都有。这儿有来自经销商的一两项建议，相信你一定会感兴趣的。

C：是什么建议呢？有什么利于销售的吗？

L：或许吧，一般的意见认为，后座的货架最好是能够分开另外供应。

C：我想，那将会使价格降低的。我会跟我们海外部商量，听听他们对这件事情是怎

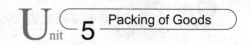

个说法。

L: 谢谢。

▶ 对话 2　劝说对方接受包装

刘小姐（L）正在劝说韦斯特先生（W）接受使用瓦楞纸板箱作为包装。

W: 刘小姐，很高兴我们已经在价格、数量、付款条件和交货日期方面达成了协议。这一次谈点什么呢？
L: 下面我要提出来供讨论的是包装问题。
W: 好吧，我们就换个议题，谈谈包装吧。我想听听你对包装的意见。
L: 我认为，不同的商品需要不同的包装。像纺织品，我们通常采用瓦楞纸板箱。
W: 你也许说得对。但是如果这批货物要转运的话，你不担心会受潮或被雨淋吗？我们希望你们能在包装问题上做出改进。
L: 不用担心。每个纸板箱都衬有防水材料的。
W: 恐怕纸板箱对海运来说不够结实吧。
L: 但是，我认为，像纺织品这类轻货，瓦楞纸板箱就够了。这批箱子比较轻，所以容易搬运。纸板箱不会和笨重的货物在一起堆放。此外，我们还用铁箍来加固。
W: 哦，刘小姐，我宁肯想稳当点。纸板箱容易被割破，还得把被盗的风险考虑进去。
L: 从另一方面来讲，撬破纸板箱是很容易被人发现的。这就使人对这种包装不敢轻举妄动。况且，我们的纸板箱是由特殊材料制成的，轻而且结实。
W: 但我仍然不放心，万一发生损坏或偷盗，保险公司可能会以包装不当而拒绝赔偿。
L: 你不必担心。这种纸板箱够结实了，能够适合海运，国际贸易中广泛采用这种纸板箱来包装这种货物。保险公司也不可能以此为理由拒绝赔偿的。
W: 好吧，刘小姐，如果你可以担保这一点，我们是很乐意接受纸板箱的包装的。
L: 哦，韦斯特先生，你不觉得还是最好把这个问题向保险公司提出来吗？我们所能做到的是保证包装得适合海运，但是除此之外的任何事情我们都不能承担责任。

▶ 对话 3　应对商标问题

汤姆（T）和陈（C）正在商讨怎样应对联邦食品管理局对食品商标的规定。

T: 我想一开始就讲清楚，商标问题是我们自己的问题。
C: 我告诉你，这是我们过去还没有碰到过的问题。
T: 联邦食品管理局对进口到美国的食品执行了一整套的规定，多少年来这些规定弄得既死板又烦琐，对我们进口商来说，简直使人头痛。

C: 依我看,过分严格的规定只不过是限制进口的一种形式。

T: 哦,有点道理。根据当前联邦食品管理局的规定,现在使用的"马玲"商标不能用于进口到美国去的荔枝。

C: 为什么不能呢?我们的罐头荔枝和其他罐头食品在世界各地市场上已经广泛销售,而"马玲"商标已为大多数国外客户和进口商所接受。难道你们不能使用现在的"马玲"商标吗?

T: 如果能够这么做,那我们是很愿意的。但我们必须遵守根据我们的法律所制定的商标规定,否则,我们的这批荔枝在海关就无法通过。

C: 那样的话,我们能帮你些什么呢?你有什么建议?

T: 你能否考虑报给我们一批中性商标的罐头,以 CIF 香港交货价为基础。我们在那儿的联号将把符合联邦食品管理局规定的商标印在上面。

C: 你认为那是唯一的办法吗?你知道,我们通常自己贴商标的,因为我们要对我们产品的牌子负责。

T: 但现在的商标不行,你是否能说服马玲工厂为我们印上其他不同的商标呢?

C: 我想,只要你们的要求合理,他们是可以考虑的。

T: 这太好了,我别无祈求。

▶ 对话 4　药品包装

李女士(L)正在向格林先生(G)介绍药品的包装。

G: 李女士,您好!

L: 您好,格林先生,欢迎你来中国。

G: 谢谢!我很高兴能再次来中国。

L: 请坐!听说你想了解药品的包装情况,是吗?

G: 对。我这次来主要想看看包装的样品,因为这关系到我们的销售。

L: 是的。商品的包装也直接关系到我们产品的声誉,因此,我们也非常重视。

G: 几年前我们买了一批药品,就是因为包装太差,影响了销售,造成了损失。

L: 格林先生,那是个别情况。你再看看我们现在的包装,你一定会认为这些包装非常美观和讲究。

G: 让我看看好吗?

L: 当然,这儿是样品间。以片剂为例。塑料瓶包装,十瓶装入一盒。旅游者携带也方便。用完药,药盒还是一件工艺品呢。

G: 太好了,真没想到你们的包装这么好。针剂怎么包装呢?

L: 大部分用塑料瓶装,小部分用玻璃瓶装。十支装入一盒,二百盒装入一个纸箱,纸

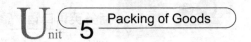

箱里面还垫有泡沫塑料。就是发生挤压碰撞也坏不了。
G: 好，很好！中药丸剂怎么包装呢？
L: 先把丸剂装入小盒，用蜡密封。然后，十小盒装入一个长方形的锦缎盒，盒外边系有一条漂亮的绸带。
G: 真漂亮！现在贵国商品的包装比以前讲究多了，那包装费由谁支付呢？
L: 由买方支付。包装费大约占货物总值的5%。通常，售价里已经包括了包装费，我们的这次交易也是如此。
G: 只要能保证质量，安全运到，售价稍高点儿也没关系。
L: 你真是个行家，包装方面还有什么问题或要求吗？
G: 没有了。看了样品，我心里就有底了。感谢你的详细介绍。

Extended Reading

Packing Containers

Generally we divide packing into transport packing(or outer packing) and sales packing (or inner packing). Deals should choose different packing containers according to the material of the goods.

Bag: may be made of strong paper, linen, canvas, rubber, etc.

Sack: a large bag of strong, coarse material for holding objects in bulk, commonly used for power and granular materials.

Carton: made of light but strong cardboard or fiberboard, widely used in export packing because it is light, cheap and resilient. The carton is double walled or triple walled.

Case: a strong container made of wood used for small, heavy items.

Box: a small case, which may be made of wood, cardboard or metal.

Crate: a slatted wooden case not fully enclosed, used for storing or shipping, usually used for large and heavy objects like machines.

Drum: a cylinder-shaped container for carrying liquids, chemicals, paints, powers, etc., made of metal, wood or cardboard.

Topic discussion:

Briefly explain the forms of packing containers.

其他常用词汇和短语

bag/sack n. 袋
barrel n. 琵琶桶，粗腰桶
basket n. 篮，篓，筐
be in bad order 破损，(包装) 不合格
be in good order 完好
bottle n. 瓶
box n. 盒
bundle n. 捆，束
can/tin n. 罐，听
canvas n. 帆布
carton n. 纸板箱，纸箱
case/chest n. 箱
cask n. 桶
casket n. 小箱
cellophane n. 玻璃纸
chest n. 箱
coil n. 捆，卷
collective packing 组合包装
consumer pack/packing 零售包装，消费包装
container n. 集装箱
corrosive n. 腐蚀性物品
crate n. 板条箱
customary packing 习惯包装，惯用包装
cylinder n. 铁桶，汽缸
drum n. 圆桶
explosive n. 爆炸品

fireworks n. 礼花
fragile n. 易碎品
handle with care 小心轻放
hanging packing 挂式包装
hogshead n. 大桶
intact a. 完整的，未损伤的
inflammable n. 易燃物
keep away from boilers 远离锅炉
keep away from cold 请勿受冷
keep away from heat 请勿受热
keep dry 保持干燥
keep in a cool place 在冷处保管
keg n. 小桶
mark n. 标志，唛头
package n. 包装（指包、捆、束、箱等），包裹
packing n. 包装（法）
packing and presentation 包装及外观
packing charge/expense 包装费用
packing clause 包装条款
packing cost 包装成本
packing credit 打包放款，包装信用证
packing extra 包装费用另计
packet n. 小包
pallet n. 托盘
parcel n. 小包，一批货
poison n. 毒剂
polythene n. 聚乙烯

Unit 6
Shipment of Goods
货物装运

Learning Resources

Warming-up

Shipment is very important in foreign trade because goods sold by the seller have to be delivered to the buyer abroad, and the delivery of goods is made possible by shipping service. Shipment, one of the indispensable terms of sales contract, signifies the seller's fulfillment of the obligation to make delivery of the goods. In practice, shipment involves such procedures as clearing the goods through the customs, booking shipping space or chartering a ship, completing shipping documentation, dispatching shipping advice. There are three parties involved in the movement of goods: the consignor or the shipper (who sends goods), the carrier (who carries the goods), and the consignee (who receives the goods at the destination).

Dialogues

Dialogue 1 Urging Delivery

Mr. Brown (B) and Ms. Abby (A) are negotiating to deliver the goods in advance.

A: Now we have settled the terms of payment. Is it possible to effect shipment during September?

B: I don't think we can.

A: Then when is the earliest we can expect shipment?

B: By the middle of October, I think.

A: That's too late. You see, November is the season for this commodity in our market, and our customs formalities are rather complicated.

B: I understand.

A: Besides, the flow through the marketing channels and the red tape involved take at least a couple of weeks. Thus, after shipment it will be four to five weeks altogether before the goods can reach our retailers. The goods must therefore be shipped before October; otherwise we won't be in time for the selling season.

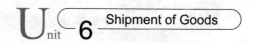

B: But our factories are fully committed for the third quarter. In fact, many of our clients are placing orders for delivery in the fourth quarter.

A: Mr. Brown, you certainly realize that the time of delivery is a matter of great importance to us. If we place our goods on the market at a time when all other importers have already sold their goods at profitable prices, we shall lose out.

B: I see your point. However, we have done more business this year than any of the previous years. I am very sorry to say that we cannot advance the time of delivery.

A: That's too bad, but I sincerely hope you will give our request your special consideration.

B: You may take it from me that the last thing we want to do is to disappoint an old customer like you. But the fact remains that our manufacturers have a heavy backlog on their hands.

A: But can't you find some way to get round your producers for an earlier delivery? Make a special effort, please. A timely delivery means a lot to us.

B: All right. We'll get in touch with our producers and see what they have to say.

Dialogue 2   Deciding the Port of Shipment

Mr. Jackson (J) wants to have the goods shipped from New York to Osaka via Hong Kong, where they can be transshipped. So he wants to make Hong Kong the port of shipment instead of New York, and Ms. Smith (S) suggests Seattle as port of shipment.

J: It has just occurred to me that there is still another possibility to ensure a prompt delivery of the goods.

S: And that is?

J: How about making Hong Kong the port of shipment instead of New York?

S: I'm afraid we can't agree to that. We concluded the business with you here in Houston, and the goods you ordered are manufactured in New York. We wish to point out that all orders accepted by us are shipped from New York or Seattle. Hong Kong is out of the question.

J: It's like this. There are only one or two ships sailing a month from New York to Osaka, while sailings from Hong Kong are quite frequent. If shipment were effected from Hong Kong, we could receive the goods much earlier.

S: I see. You want to have your goods shipped from New York to Osaka via Hong Kong, where they can be transshipped. Is that the idea?

J: Yes, exactly, because I want these goods on our market at the earliest possible date.

S: Your idea may be a good one, but the trouble is that there are risks of pilferage or damage to the goods during transshipment at Hong Kong. How about shipping them from Seattle instead of New York? You may choose either one as port of shipment. It makes no difference to us. There are more sailings from Seattle than from New York.

J: It sounds all right to me, but I will have to think about it. I'll give you a definite answer tomorrow. If I choose Seattle, will it be possible for you to ship the goods by the end of March?

S: We'll try our best. Anyway, we assure you that shipment will be made not later than the first half of April.

Dialogue 3 Confirming the Time of Shipment

Ms. Jones (J) is confirming the time of shipment with Mr. Wang (W).

· J: Could you do something to advance your time of shipment?

W: Well, our manufacturers are fully committed at the moment. I'm afraid it's very difficult to improve any further on the time.

· J: I hope you'll try to convince them to step up production.

W: We check their production schedule against our orders almost every day. As new orders keep coming in, they are working three shifts to step up production. I'm sorry, but we simply can not commit ourselves beyond what the production schedule can fulfill.

· J: Well, in that case, there is nothing more to be said. What's your last word as to the date then?

W: I said by the middle of October. This is the best we can promise.

· J: All right. I'll take you at your word. May I suggest that you put down in the contract shipment on October 15th or earlier? Our letter of credit will be opened in early September.

W: Good. Let's call it a deal. We'll do our best to advance the shipment to September. The chances are that some of the other orders may be cancelled. But of course you cannot count on that. In any case, we'll let you know by e-mail.

· J: That's very considerate of you. And now, shall we discuss the insurance terms?

W: We generally insure WP (WPA) on a CIF offer. Special risks, such as TPND (theft, pilferage and non-delivery), leakage, breakage, oil, freshwater, etc. can also be covered upon request.

· J: I suppose the additional premium for the special coverage is for the buyer's account.

W: Quite right. According to the usual practice in international trade, special risks are not covered unless the buyer asks for them.

- **J:** Then what about SRCC (Strikes, Riots and Civil Commotions)? Can we request you to cover this for our imports?
- **W:** Yes, we accept it now, after it has been suspended for many years. However, if you want to have it covered for your imports at your end, you may arrange the insurance as you like.
- **J:** Then please cover WPA and TPND for this transaction.
- **W:** All right, I'll adjust the price accordingly.

Dialogue 4 Hoping to Allow Partial Shipment

Miss Lee (L), the seller, hopes Mr. West (W) to allow partial shipment in order to get the goods ready for the shipment.

- **L:** Now that we have reached an agreement on the packing, we can come to the next problem — shipment. What's your opinion, Mr. West?
- **W:** That's good. Would you tell me how you ship the goods?
- **L:** We usually ship the goods by regular liners.
- **W:** For this lot, could you consider prompt shipment?
- **L:** No, I'm afraid it's difficult for us to do so because we can't get all the goods from our manufacturers soon.
- **W:** When is the exact deadline of the loading period?
- **L:** In order to make it easier for us to get the goods ready for the shipment, we hope that partial shipment will be allowed.
- **W:** The goods we have ordered are seasonal goods, so it will be better to ship them all at one time.
- **L:** Sorry, we can't ship them all at one time because it so happens that there is no direct steamer from here to your port in these two months. I was informed by our shipping department yesterday that liner space for America up to the end of next month has been fully booked. I'm afraid we can do very little about it.
- **W:** It is said that tramps are still available.
- **L:** Yes, but the tramps are scarce. I'm not sure whether there would be enough tonnage to make a full cargo, even if a tramp could be obtained.

Words and Expressions

to effect shipment (= to make shipment) 装运（effect 意为"实现"）
the season for this commodity 这个商品的销售季节
customs n. 海关，关税
formality n. 正式手续
red tape 烦琐的官方手续
retailer n. 零售店，零售商
season n. 季节，旺季
place our goods on the market (push the sale of our goods) 销售商品
lose out 输掉，亏本
You may take it from me... 我可以向你保证……
the last thing we want to do 我们最不想做的事是……
backlog n. 待办事项
Osaka n. 大阪（日本地名）
via Hong Kong 途经香港
transship v. 转运，换船
pilferage n. （小量地）偷
production schedule 生产进度表

to step up production 加快生产
cannot commit ourselves... 我们不能保证……，我们无法承诺……
Let's call it a deal. （口）这笔交易就敲定（拍板）吧。
The chances are... (probably) 可能是……
You cannot count on that. 你不要指望那个。
insure v. 为……投保
special risk 特种险
theft, pilferage and non-delivery (TPND) 偷窃提货不着险
leakage n. 漏损（险）
breakage n. 破损（险）
freshwater n. 淡水（险）
coverage n. （保险合同所列的）险别
for the buyer's account 由买方负担费用
at your end/on your side 在你方
regular liner 班机，班船
prompt shipment 即期装运
the exact deadline of the loading period 确切的装船期限
direct steamer (vessel) 直达船

Notes

1. 定程船舶（liner）

定程船舶也称班轮，是指在海洋运输中，在一个固定的航线上按照预定日期，经常来往于若干目的港口，承运旅客及（或）货物的轮船。这种轮船又可分为定期货轮、定

Unit 6 Shipment of Goods

期客轮和定期客货轮。

2. 海关（customs）

海关是根据国家法令，对进出国境的货物、邮递物品、旅客行李、货币、金银、证券和运输工具等进行监督和检查，征收关税，并执行查禁走私任务的国家行政管理机关。

3. 关税（tariff）

商品通过国境时，向海关交纳的税金，称为关税。关税按性质分，有三种：对进口商品征收的进口税；对出口商品征收的出口税；对过境商品征收的过境税、转口税和通关税。

4. 联运（multi-model combined transport）

进出口贸易的货物运输，常常不是一种方式所能完成的，而是需要多种方式结合进行。在陆、海、空三种运输的基础上，择优发展形成的综合运输方式，就叫作联运或联合运输。

5. 非定期轮船（tramp）

非定期轮船无固定航线和预订的船期，哪儿能揽到货运，就往哪儿航行，或供包租。

6. 任意港（free port）

国际贸易中货运目的港并不限定一个。除价格条件中规定的目的港外，买方还可以指定第二目的港、第三目的港，甚至第四目的港。此种港口，国际贸易术语称"任意港"。任意港必须是原定航线沿途必经的寄航港。

7. 租船（charter）

进出口商如有大量货物待运，可租船装运。租费的计算有两种，一是按时间计费，一是按航次计费。

8. 托盘运输（pallet shipment）

货物在生产地装好托盘一起托运，直到收货人。其间运转也是机械操作，省时省费，又能减少运输中的错发、错运、多装、少装等现象。

Useful Sentences

1. How long does it usually take you to make a delivery?
   通常你方需要多长时间交货？
2. As a rule, we deliver all our orders within three months after receipt of the covering L/C.
   一般说来，我们在收到有关的信用证后三个月内可交货。
3. Could you possibly advance shipment further more?
   你方能不能再提前一点交货呢？

4. I hope that the goods can be shipped promptly after you get our L/C.
   我希望你们能在收到我方信用证后马上装运。
5. Shipment should be made before October, otherwise we are not able to catch the season.
   十月底前必须交货，否则就赶不上销售季节了。
6. The earliest shipment we can make is early March.
   三月初是我们能够做到的最早交货日期。
7. I'm sorry, we can't advance the time of shipment.
   很抱歉，我们不能提前交货。
8. The order is so urgently required that we must ask you to expedite shipment.
   我方迫切需要这次订货，故请贵方加快装运。
9. We are confident of being able to ship the goods to you by the end of next month.
   我们相信能在下月底前将货物装运给你们。
10. The goods ordered are all in stock and we assure you that the first steamer will make the shipment available in November.
    贵公司订购的货物我方均有现货，可保证在十一月份将货物装上第一条轮船。
11. Please see to it that the goods are shipped per PEACE sailing on or about October 15th.
    请确保货物由10月15日左右启航的"和平轮"装运。
12. Shipment by the middle of October will be too late for us.
    十月中旬交货太晚了。
13. We'll try our best to advance shipment to September.
    我们会尽最大努力将交货期提前到九月。
14. When is the earliest possible date you can ship the goods?
    你们最早什么时候可以装运呢？
15. I wonder whether you can make shipment in September.
    我想知道你们能否在九月份装运。
16. How long will the delivery take from here to Canada by sea freight?
    从这里到加拿大海运需多长时间？
17. I don't think I can promise you any January shipments.
    我不能保证一月份发货。
18. Please be informed that the shipment of the cargo (your purchase order No. 123) was sent yesterday, airway bill No. 123.
    特此通知这批货物（你方订单号码是123）昨天已装运，航空运单号码是123。
19. In case you do not receive the goods on or before December 12, please let us know.
    万一你方没有在12月12日或之前收到货物，请告知我方。

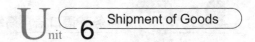

20. We will do all we can to fill your order so that the goods will be shipped before October 15.
    我方将尽全力履行此订单，并于 10 月 15 日前安排这些货物装船。

I **Complete the following dialogues.**

1. **A:** _____?
   （能告诉我你们什么时候可以交货吗？）
   B: Our earliest time of delivery is October.

2. **A:** Could you deliver 100 tons immediately?
   B: _____.
   （没问题。我们可以交现货来满足你们的要求。）

3. **A:** Please ship the goods in one lot in May.
   B: I'm sorry that's impossible. _____.
   （那么短的时间把货物准备好对我们来说很难。）

4. **A:** _____?
   （你能不能想办法提前装运？）
   B: May I suggest we effect shipment in three equal lots, starting from May?

5. **A:** Our people are most anxious about the October shipment; so far they've heard nothing from you.
   B: We're sorry for the delay. _____.
   （问题是直达你们港口的船只太少了。）

II **Situational practice.**

The situation: Mr. Smith requests to advance the shipment as his client is in urgent need of the goods. The seller regrets being unable to ship the goods as requested. Mr. Smith allows partial shipment and the seller promises to contact the factory.

  The task: Create a dialogue according to the situation.

国际商务英语口语 高级

对话汉译

▶ **对话1** 催促发货

布朗先生（B）和阿比女士（A）正在商谈提前发货。

A：现在我们已经谈妥了付款条件，你方是否能够在九月份装船？
B：我看不行。
A：那么最早什么时候可以装船呢？
B：恐怕要在十月中旬。
A：那太迟了。你知道，在我方市场上，十一月份是这种商品的上市季节，而且我们的海关手续又相当复杂。
B：我明白。
A：另外，通过销售渠道以及烦琐的公文程序，起码要花上几个星期。这样从装船后到我们的零售商收到货物，总共要用四五个星期。因此，十月份前货物必须装船，否则我们就赶不上销售季节了。
B：但是我们工厂第三季度的生产任务已全部排满了。事实上，我们很多客户在订第四季度交的货呢。
A：布朗先生，你知道的，交货时间对我们来说很重要。如果在我们把商品投放到市场上去的时候，别的进口商已经把商品脱手赚钱了，那我们就亏了。
B：这点我明白。但是今年我们的业务比往年都要多。很遗憾不能提前交货。
A：那糟了，但我真心希望你们对我们的要求给予特殊的考虑。
B：我可以向你保证，我们最不愿做的事就是让像你们这样的老客户失望，但是我们的厂家眼前的交货压得很重，这是事实。
A：你能想些办法说服厂家提前一些时间交货吗？请你多费些心。及时交货对我们关系可大啦！
B：好吧。我们和厂家联系一下，听听他们的意见。

▶ **对话2** 决定交货港

杰克逊先生（J）希望经由香港中转把货从纽约运到大阪，所以他希望把交货港由纽约改为香港。史密斯女士（S）建议把西雅图作为交货港。

J: 我刚想起来了,还有一种可能性确保即期交货。

S: 什么可能性?

J: 把交货港从纽约改为香港怎么样?

S: 那个我们恐怕不能同意。我们是在休斯敦达成交易的,而你所订货物在纽约生产。我们要指出的是,我们接受的所有订货是从纽约或西雅图发货的。香港不行。

J: 原因是这样的:从纽约到大阪每个月只有一两个航班,而从香港到大阪的航班却相当频繁。如果在香港交货,我们收到货物的时间就会早很多。

S: 原来是这样。你想经由香港中转把货从纽约运到大阪,是不是?

J: 对,就是这样,因为我们想把商品尽可能早地投放市场。

S: 这个想法倒不错。不过问题是,在香港转船期间,货物有被偷窃和损坏的风险。交货港由纽约改为西雅图怎么样?你可以随便选择一个装运港。对我们来说都一样。从西雅图启航的船只比纽约多。

J: 我觉得不错,但我得想一想,明天给你答复。如果我选择西雅图,你们能在三月底前交货吗?

S: 我们尽力而为吧!不管怎样,请你放心,交货不会迟于四月上旬。

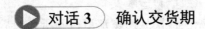 对话 3　确认交货期

琼斯女士(J)正在和王先生(W)确认交货期

J: 你们能否想些办法提前交货呢?

W: 我们的厂家目前承单较多,要再提前恐怕很难。

J: 希望你们能设法说服他们加速生产。

W: 我们几乎每天核对他们的生产进度以跟进订单。由于不断地收到新订单,他们现在一天三班工作来加快生产。很抱歉,我们承担的任务实在无法超出生产计划所能完成的限额。

J: 如果是这样,多说也无益。那么你能不能最后确定一下什么时候能交货呢?

W: 要到十月中旬,这是我们能够答应的最好条件了。

J: 好吧,那就以你的话为准了。建议你在合同里写上"10月15日或之前交货"行吗?我们会在9月初开立信用证。

W: 好!就这样决定吧!我们尽力把交货期提前到九月份。有可能取消其他一些订单,不过当然还不确定。不管怎样,我们会发电子邮件告知你的。

J: 你想得真周到。现在我们谈谈保险条款好吗?

W: 一般来讲,我们在到岸价里投保了水渍险。特殊险如偷窃险、提货不着险、漏损险、破损险、油污险、淡水险等也可以根据客户要求投保。

J: 我想投保特殊险别所需附加的保险费由买方负担吧。
W: 正是，根据国际贸易中的惯例，只有买方要求时才保特殊险。
J: 那么关于罢工、暴动、平民动乱险呢？能不能请你方为我们的进口货投保这种险呢？
W: 我们现在可以受理了，很多年来我们停办了这项业务。但是如果你方想要为你们的进口货物投保这种险的话，你们可以自行安排。
J: 那么，请为这批货物保水渍险和偷窃、提货不着险。
W: 好的，我会相应地把价格调整一下。

对话 4　希望买方允许分批装运

卖方李小组（L）为了准备货物，希望韦斯特先生（W）允许分批装运。

L: 我们既然在包装问题上达成了协议，可以讨论下一个问题——装运问题了。韦斯特先生，你意下如何？
W: 那好。你们打算如何装运这批货物呢？
L: 我们一般采用定期装运。
W: 对于我们这批货，能否考虑即期装运呢？
L: 恐怕很难办理，因为我们无法很快从厂家那里得到所有的货物。
W: 我们这批货物装船的最后期限究竟是什么时候呢？
L: 为了方便准备装船货物，希望你们允许分批装船。
W: 我们订购的这批货物是季节性商品，还是一次发运为好。
L: 对不起，我们无法一次发运，因为碰巧这两个月内没有从这里驶往你方港口的直达船。昨天我们的运输部门告诉我，下个月底前开往美国的班船舱位已全部订满，恐怕我们也无能为力了。
W: 据说不定期的货轮还是有的。
L: 有的，不过很少。即使有了这样一条不定期的货轮，我也不敢担保是否有足够的吨位装运全部货物。

Extended Reading

Preparing the Goods for Shipment

After an offer is accepted by the importer or an order is confirmed by the exporter, the business or the transaction is considered closed. The exporter will go ahead to prepare the

Unit 6　Shipment of Goods

goods for shipment and book shipping space if the term is CIF or CFR. Shipment is an important part in international business. Goods are carried by several means of conveyance—on road or rail, by sea or air and in recent years, combined transport which is a road-sea-rail carriage has appeared. When goods are transported by road, rail or air, the contract of carriage takes the form of a consignment note or air way bill. In sea transport, chartering of ships or booking shipping space is involved. And the contract entered into between the ship-owner and shipper may take the form of either a charter party or a bill of landing.

Topic discussion:

Are there any other modes of transportation with which you are familiar? Try to compare their advantages and disadvantages with marine transportation.

其他常用词汇和短语

additional charge/fee　额外费用
airway bill　航空运单
bill of lading (B/L)　提单
book shipping space　订舱位
cargo receipt　货物收据
charge a ship　租船
charter party　租船契约，租船人（团体）
commercial invoice　商业发票
consignee　n. 收货人
consigner　n. 发货人
cost of transportation　运输费
demurrage　n. 滞期费
delay shipment　延误装运
deliver goods　发货
delivery　n. 交货
delivery in installments　分批装运

direct shipment　直接装运
dispatch goods　发货
dispatch money　速遣费
European main ports (EMP)　欧洲主要口岸
estimated time of arrival (ETA)　预抵期
estimated time of departure (ETD)　预离期
effect shipment　完成装运
express shipment　快速装运
freight charge　运费
freight collect　运费到付
freight prepaid　运费预付
hasten shipment　加快装运
immediate delivery　立刻交货
lay days　受载日期，装卸时间
liner　n. 定期轮船，班轮

mode of transportation 运输方式	on board B/L) 装船提单
non-negotiable B/L 不可转让提单	shipping company 运输公司
on deck B/L 舱面提单	shipping documents 装运单据
optional port 任意港	shipping mark 唛头
order B/L 指示提单	stale B/L 过期提单
partial shipment 分批装运	straight B/L 记名提单
port of destination 目的港	through B/L 联运提单
port of loading 装货港	time of shipment 装运期
port of shipment 装运港	timely shipment 及时装运
port of unloading/discharge 卸货港	tramp n. 非定期轮船
punctual delivery 按期交货	transshipment B/L 转船提单
shipping advice 装船通知	unclean B/L (dirty B/L, foul B/L) 不清洁提单
shipping agent 装运代理商	
shipped B/L (on board B/L, shipped	

Unit 7

Inspection, Quarantine and Checking of Goods
货物检验、检疫及验收

Learning Resources

Warming-up

Commodity inspection, quarantine, and checking is very important in the foreign trade. Commodity inspection is the practice and formalities involved in physical inspection coupled with collecting, presenting, communicating and processing data required for the movement of goods in international trade. But to the national governments, trade inspection and security is the act of monitoring and reviewing specific trade activity for the purpose of determining compliance with regulatory requirements while at the same time ensuring the security of goods and the nation.

There are mainly two required inspection of goods in international trade, namely: pre-shipment inspection of goods and destination inspection of goods. Pre-shipment inspection is a service provided by inspection institute to verify that the price, exchange rate, financial terms, quantity, quality and customs classification of the transaction are consistent with what was ordered. The inspection is done physically and is usually done in the goods country of origin before effecting shipment. Destination Inspection is a service whereby goods and import declarations are inspected on arrival in the importing country. It is important to note that the goods are not physically inspected as is done in pre-shipment. Destination inspection represents an efficient and effective tool for governments, customs authorities and traders to combine the facilitation of legitimate trade with the need for responsible enforcement.

In many cases, the buyer may be well advised to arrange for inspection of the goods before or at the time they are handed over by the seller for carriage (so-called pre-shipment inspection or PSI). Unless the contract stipulates otherwise, the buyer would himself have to pay the cost for such inspection that is arranged in his own interest. However, if the inspection has been made in order to enable the seller to comply with any mandatory rules applicable to the export of the goods in his own country, the seller would have to pay for that inspection, unless the EXW term used, in which case the costs of such inspection are for the account of the buyer.

Objects subject to entry-exit inspection and quarantine include commodities (including animal and plant products), and means of transportation and transport equipment carrying commodities, animals, plants and passengers in and out of a country, as well as persons entering and exiting the country.

Unit 7 Inspection, Quarantine and Checking of Goods

Dialogues

▶ Dialogue 1   The Entry-Exit Declaration

Mr. Wilson (W) is at the entry-exit declaration office. He is asking the officer (O) the procedures and the material required to deliver goods.

W: Morning.

O: Morning. What are you going to transport, Mr. Wilson?

W: A batch of refined flours.

O: Please apply to the entry-exit inspection and quarantine institution for inspection ten days before you ship for export.

W: Can you tell me which kinds of certificates I should provide?

O: The foreign trade contract or order form, letter of credit (L/C), receipts and the departure of your goods from port.

W: Thank you so much.

O: You're welcome.

▶ Dialogue 2   Talking about the Inspection and Checking of the Exported Goods

Mr. Li (L) is discussing with Ms. Edward (E) about commodity inspection to make sure of the goods' quality and safety.

L: You mean you sell on shipped quality, quantity, and weight?

E: That's right. The goods will be inspected by the Britain Import and Export Commodity Inspection Bureau. It will then issue a certificate of quality and a certificate of weight. These will be taken as final and binding.

L: But in the case of short weight or disqualification?

E: I assure you that is not likely to happen. Our goods must be up to the export standards before the inspection bureau releases them.

L: The transaction involves frozen food; we have to make sure the sanitary standards are up to the requirements of Chinese government.

E: Our inspection bureau will issue a veterinary inspection certificate to show that the shipment is in conformity with the Euro export standards.
L: I see. Thanks a lot.
E: It's my pleasure to help you.

Dialogue 3 Inspection and Reinspection of the Goods

Ms. Liu (L) is discussing with Mr. Green (G) inspection and checking of goods while trying to make an agreement.

L: Now, let's talk about the clause of inspection.
G: Yeah, that's another crucial part of the contract.
L: The exporters have the right to inspect the goods before shipment and the importers have the right to reinspect the goods after their arrival.
G: The exporters bear the inspection fee and the importers bear the reinspection fee. Is it right?
L: That's it.
G: Which organization is in charge of the reinspection?
L: The China Import and Export Commodity Bureau or any of its branches which will issue the inspection certificate.
G: What's the time limit for inspection?
L: Sixty days after the arrival of goods in Qingdao.
G: What if the result of the reinspection does not coincide with that of the inspection?
L: The goods won't be accepted. All the losses and expenses should be borne by the seller.
G: You know. Anything can happen to the goods in the long distance delivery.
L: I see. How do you clarify the responsibilities?
G: We can hold a seminar of technical specialists as well as the surveyors from both sides to make a decision.
L: That's good.
G: We hope to deal with differences through friendly negotiations.
L: We are the same.

Dialogue 4 Inspection and Checking of the Goods

Mr. Edward (E) plans to import machines and equipment used in production of tires. He is discussing the questions of goods inspection with Ms. Chen (C), the exporter.

Unit 7 Inspection, Quarantine and Checking of Goods

C: Good afternoon, Mr. Edward.

E: Good afternoon, Ms. Chen. Shall we go down to the question of inspection?

C: That's what we're here for. Now please go ahead.

E: We demand that before delivery you should test and inspect all the equipment and parts comprehensively in regard to quality, quantity, specification and performance and issue a test report along with the certificate of inspection issued by the inspection agency which is approved by both parties and stipulated in the contract.

C: We certainly will. Actually, it is our usual practice to inspect all the equipment and parts before shipment.

E: After the equipment has been transported to the job site, it must be carefully checked and inspected by our representative and the Singaporean Commodity Inspection Bureau. You can dispatch your representative to join the open-package inspection, if you like.

C: We will. Please inform us of the date of inspection one month before the open-package inspection.

E: We will. During inspection, if shortages, defects or anything which doesn't conform to the contract are found, we will be entitled to claim against you.

C: We agree. But if any damage of goods will be found due to the responsibilities of the insurance company or the shipping company, we won't assume any responsibility.

E: In that event, we'll want you to replace the damaged goods as soon as you receive our notice. Of course, the expenses thus incurred shall not be at your account.

C: OK.

E: But if we find any discrepancy which falls within your responsibility, the Singaporean Commodity Inspection Bureau will issue a certificate which will be the effective evidence for us to claim payment from you.

C: I agree.

Words and Expressions

a batch of 一批
apply to 向……申请（要求）
entry-exit inspection and quarantine institution 进出口检验检疫机构
the foreign trade contract 对外贸易合同
order form 订货单
letter of credit (L/C) （银行发行的）信用证
shipped quality, quantity, and weight 装货质量、数量和重量
issue a certificate 出具证明

final and binding 最后的依据并具有约束力	和……一致（符合），遵照
short weight 重量不足	clause n. （合同的）条款
disqualification n. 质量不合格	in charge of 负责
be likely to 可能	time limit 期限
sanitary standards 卫生标准	coincide with 与……一致
veterinary inspection certificate 动物检疫证明书	long distance delivery 长距离运输
	job site 现场
	dispatch v. 派遣
in conformity with 和……相适应，	open-package inspection 开箱检验

Notes

1. 什么是商品检验

商品检验是指商品的产方、买方或者第三方在一定条件下，借助于某种手段和方法，按照合同、标准或国内外有关法律、法规、惯例，对商品的质量、规格、重量、数量、包装、安全及卫生等方面进行检查，并做出合格与否或通过验收与否的判定或为维护买卖双方合法权益，避免或解决各种风险损失和责任划分的争议，便于商品交接结算而出具各种有关证书的业务活动。

2. 商品检验的作用

商品检验可以作为报关验放的有效证件；买卖双方结算货款的依据；计算运输、仓储等费用的依据；办理索赔的依据；计算关税的依据；作为证明情况、明确责任的证件；作为仲裁、诉讼举证的有效文件。

3. 商品检验的形式

接受检验商品的数量不同，可分为全数检验、抽样检验和免于检验。全数检验，又称全额检验、百分之百检验，是对整批商品逐个（件）地进行的检验。其特点是能提供较多的质量信息，给人一种心理上的放心感。缺点是由于检验量大，其费用高，易造成检验人员疲劳而导致漏检或错检。抽样检验，是按照已确定的抽样方案，从整批商品中随机抽取少量商品用作逐一测试的样品，并依据测试结果去推断整批商品质量合格与否的检验。它具有占用人力、物力和时间少的优点，具有一定的科学性和准确性，是比较经济的检验方式。但检验结果相对于整批商品实际质量水平，总会有一定误差。免于检验，即对于生产技术水平高和检验条件好、质量管理严格、成品质量长期稳定的企业生产出来的商品，在企业自检合格后，商业和外贸部门可以直接收货，免于检验。

Unit 7 Inspection, Quarantine and Checking of Goods

4. 进出口商品检验和鉴定的工作程序

一般来讲，大致要经过接受报检，抽样制样，检验拟稿，签证放行等环节。具体就是由具有申请检验资格的单位，按照申请检验鉴定的工作项目，填写报验单，提供应附的有关单证，在限定的时间内到当地的商检机构申请检验，商检机构受理报验申请后，经专业检验人员经过一系列的抽样、制样以及检验鉴定工作，拟制检验鉴定结果证稿，最后签发相应的检验或鉴定证明书。

5. 商品检验的内容

（1）品质检验。品质检验是根据合同和有关检验标准规定或申请人的要求对商品的使用价值所表现出来的各种特性、运用人的感官或化学、物理的等各种手段进行测试、鉴别。其目的就是判别、确定该商品的质量是否符合合同中规定的商品质量条件。品质检验包括外观品质和内在品质的检验。

外观品质检验：是指对商品外观尺寸、造型、结构、款式、表面色彩、表面精度、软硬度、光泽度、新鲜度、成熟度、气味等的检验；内在品质检验：是指对商品的化学组成、性质和等级等技术指标的检验。

（2）规格检验。规格表示同类商品在量（如体积、容积、面积、粗细、长度、宽度、厚度等）方面的差别，与商品品质优次无关。如鞋类的大小、纤维的长度和粗细、玻璃的厚度和面积等规格，只表明商品之间在量上的差别，而商品品质取决于品质条件。商品规格是确定规格差价的依据。由于商品的品质与规格是密切相关的两个质量特征，因此，贸易合同中的品质条款中一般都包括了规格要求。

（3）数量和重量检验。它们是买卖双方成交商品的基本计量和计价单位，直接关系着双方的经济利益，也是对外贸易中最敏感而且容易引起争议的因素之一。它们包括了商品个数、件数、双数、打数、令数、长度、面积、体积、容积和重量等。

（4）包装质量检验。商品包装本身的质量和完好程度，不仅直接关系着商品的质量，还关系着商品数量和重量。一旦出现问题时，是商业部门分清责任归属、确定索赔对象的重要依据之一。如检验中发现有商品数（重）量不足情况，包装破损者，责任在运输部门；包装完好者，责任在生产部门。包装质量检验的内容主要是内外包装的质量。如包装材料、容器结构、造型和装潢等对商品贮存、运输、销售的适宜性，包装体的完好程度，包装标志的正确性和清晰度，包装防护措施的牢固度等。

（5）安全、卫生检验。商品安全检验是指电子电器类商品的漏电检验，绝缘性能检验和X光辐射等。商品的卫生检验是指商品中的有毒有害物质及微生物的检验。如食品添加剂中砷、铅、镉的检验，茶叶中的农药残留量检验等。

对于进出口商品的检验内容除上述内容外，还包括海损鉴定、集装箱检验、进出口商品的残损检验、出口商品的装运技术条件检验、货载衡量、产地证明、价值证明以及其他业务的检验。

Useful Sentences

1. We will inspect this batch of sneakers to see if there are any quality problems.
   我们将检查这批球鞋看是否有质量问题。
2. I'm worried that there might be some disputes over the results of inspection.
   我担心对商检的结果会发生争议。
3. What's the time limit for the reinspection?
   复检的时限是多久呢?
4. The exporters have the right to inspect the export goods before delivery to the shipping line.
   出口商在向船运公司托运前有权检验商品。
5. Please apply to the entry-exit inspection and quarantine institution for inspection ten days before you ship for export.
   请提前 10 天向出入境检验检疫机构提出申请检验货物。
6. How should we define the inspection rights?
   商检的权力怎样加以明确呢?
7. The importers have the rights to reinspect the goods after their arrival, and the inspection should be completed within half a month after their arrival.
   进口商在到货后有权复验商品,商品检验工作应在货到后半个月内完成。
8. Shall we take up the question of inspection today?
   今天咱们讨论商品检验问题,好吗?
9. The goods must be up to export standards before the Inspection Bureau relcases them.
   货物只有在符合出口标准后,商检局才予以放行。
10. The inspection of commodity is no easy job.
    商检工作不是那么简单。
11. Mr. Cree is talking with the Chinese importer about inspecting the goods.
    克里先生与中方进口商就商品检验问题进行洽谈。
12. Where do you want to reinspect this batch of goods?
    您希望在哪复检这批商品呢?
13. You need to have certificate showing the goods to be free from radioactive contamination.
    你们需要出具足以证明货物没有受到放射线污染的证明。
14. Inspection of commodities shall cover: quality, specification, quantity, weight, packing and requirements for safety and sanitation.

Unit 7 Inspection, Quarantine and Checking of Goods

商品检验范围包括：质量、规格、数量、重量、包装、安全和卫生要求。

15. As an integral part of the contract, the inspection of goods has its special importance.
    作为合同里的一个组成部分，商品检验具有特殊的重要性。
16. We should inspect this batch of motorcycles to see if there is any breakage.
    我们要检查一下这批摩托车是否有破损的。
17. We'll accept the goods only if the results from the two inspections are identical with each other.
    如果双方的检测结果一致，我们就收货。
18. What if the results from the inspection and the reinspection do not coincide with each other?
    如果检验和复验的结果有出入该怎么办呢？
19. The reinspection fee shall be borne by the buyers.
    复检费应由买方承担。
20. During inspection, if shortage, defects or anything which doesn't conform to the contract, we will be entitled to claim you.
    检查过程中，如果发现货物有缺少、缺陷或任何与合同规定不符的情况，我方有权向贵方提出索赔。

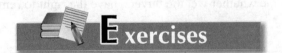

Exercises

I Complete the following dialogues.

1. A: _____?
   （您希望在哪里复验商品呢？）
   B: The China Import and Export Commodity Bureau.
2. A: What's the time limit for the reinspection?
   B: _____.
   （商品复检工作在到货后一个月内完成。）
3. A: _____?
   （如果货物的质量与合同不符，由谁出具检验证明书呢？）
   B: The certificate will be issued by China Import and Export Commodity Inspection Bureau or by any of its branches.
4. A: _____?
   （如果货物运到后，质量不合格或者重量不足怎么办呢？）

B: I assure you that is not likely to happen. Our goods must be up to the export standards before the Inspection Bureau releases them.

5. **A:** I'm afraid there may be some disputes over the results of inspection.
   B: _____.
   （您可以在规定的时间内申请复检。）

6. **A:** Is it convenient for you to engage a surveyor?
   B: _____.
   （我们有最好的公证行。）

7. **A:** _____?
   （我们需要提供什么书面材料呢？）
   B: The materials should be with the reason why you ask for the supplement. After we verify it, we will sign and issue the supplement certificate.

8. **A:** Do you have any other questions about the inspection?
   B: _____.
   （没有什么问题了，我们同意你方的条款。）

9. **A:** What shall inspection of commodities cover?
   B: _____.
   （商品检验范围包括：质量、规格、数量、重量、包装、安全和卫生要求。）

10. **A:** Would you tell me whether we, the buyers, have the right to reinspect the goods when the goods arrive?
    B: _____.
    （根据国际通行的惯例，到货后 7 天内完成复检，30 天内可以索赔。）

II Situational practice.

The situation: Your Representative Company has a frozen shrimp deal with the USA COMMEL Food Distributor. The problem is the results of the reinspection after arrival don't coincide with the first inspection before shipment.

The task: You need to negotiate with the USA COMMEL Food Distributor Representative to find out a solution to the dispute.

Unit 7 Inspection, Quarantine and Checking of Goods

对话汉译

对话 1 申报出入境货物

威尔逊先生（W）到出入境申报办公室，询问工作人员（O）申报出口货物的程序及其所需材料。

W: 早上好。
O: 早上好。威尔逊先生，您要运输什么？
W: 一批精制面粉。
O: 请提前10天向出入境检验检疫机构提出申请检验货物。
W: 我该提供哪些证明呢？
O: 外贸合同或订货单、信用证（L/C）、收据及您出港的货物。
W: 谢谢你。
O: 不客气。

对话 2 讨论出口货物检验事宜

李先生（L）与爱德华女士（E）正在讨论商品检验的问题，以确保从英国进口的速冻食品的安全性。

L: 您的意思是说贵方售货以装货质量、数量和重量为准？
E: 是的。货物由英国进出口商品检验局进行检验，然后出具质量和重量说明书。这些证明书将是最后的依据并具有约束力。
L: 但是如果重量不足或质量不合格怎么办呢？
E: 我向您保证不会发生这种情况。我们的货物只有在符合出口标准后，商检局才会放行。
L: 这次交易的货物是速冻食品。我们必须确保它的卫生标准达到中国政府的标准。
E: 我们的商品检验局将出具动物检疫证明书以证明货物符合欧盟出口标准。
L: 我明白了，非常感谢。
E: 愿意为您效劳。

对话 3　货物检验及复检

刘女士（L）和格林先生（G）在签订合同的过程中讨论到了商品检验问题。

L：我们现在讨论一下检验的条款吧。
G：好的，商检确实是合同中关键的部分。
L：出口商在向船运公司托运之前，有权对商品进行检验。商品到达之后，进口商有复检权。
G：出口商支付初检费，进口商支付复检费，对吧？
L：是这样的。
G：复检的是什么机构呢？
L：中国进出口商品检验局或其他任何签发检验证书的分局。
G：复检的期限多长呢？
L：货到青岛港后的 60 天内。
G：如果初检和复检的结果不一致怎么办呢？
L：我们将拒收货物，所有由此引起的损失及费用将由卖方支付。
G：在长距离运输中，任何事情都可能发生。
L：我知道，那该如何确定责任呢？
G：我们可以举行一个由技术专家及双方检验人员组成的讨论会，最后做出决定。
L：好的。
G：我们希望通过友好协商解决分歧。
L：我们同样希望这样。

对话 4　货物检验

爱德华先生（E）计划进口轮胎生产线所需的机器设备，他与设备出口商陈女士（C）正在讨论货物检验问题。

C：下午好，爱德华先生。
E：下午好，陈女士，我们谈一下商品检验问题好吗？
C：我们就是为此问题过来的，请讲。
E：我们要求贵方在发货前，应对所有的设备和部件的质量、数量、规格和性能做全面检查，并出具检验报告及由双方认可且由合同规定的检验部门签发的检验证明。
C：我们当然会检验的。实际上交货前对所有的设备及部件进行检验是我们通常的做法。
E：设备运到现场后，需经我方代表及新加坡商检局详细检查，贵方愿意的话也可派代

Unit 7 Inspection, Quarantine and Checking of Goods

表参加开箱检查。

C：我们要派代表。希望你们在开箱检查前一个月，将开箱检查日期通知我们。

E：我们会的。检查过程中，如果发现货物有短重、缺陷或任何与合同规定不符的情况，我方有权向贵方提出索赔。

C：同意。但如果发现货物损坏是保险人或承运人的责任造成，我方则不承担任何责任。

E：在那种情况下，我方希望贵方收到通知后，尽快更换被损坏的货物，当然由此引起的全部费用无须贵方承担。

C：好的。

E：如果我们发现由于贵方责任而造成的问题，新加坡商检局会出具证明，该证明将是我方向贵方要求赔偿的有力证据。

C：我方同意。

Extended Reading

Export and Import Goods Inspection

1. Commercial inspection

Export and import goods examination may be requested for inspection by one contracting party or some contracting parties of goods purchase and sale contract. The requests for goods inspection may be agreed to be inscribed in the purchase and sale contract or may be a particular request of one or some contracting parties for re-determining actual export and import goods. Inspection fees are paid or agreed by the parties. Commercial inspection relates only to the goods purchasers and the goods sellers, not concerning the customs office's control, the goods samples which are sent for examination may be under or not under the control of the customs offices.

2. Examination of import goods quality

Import goods shall have to be subject to state examination in terms of quality in cases where they are of the list of goods subject to state control in quality. Goods examination may be carried out before or after goods clearance. The customs offices base on goods examination conclusions or notifications of goods examination registration for carrying out customs procedures and goods clearance. In cases where the goods do not meet the requirements of import quality, the customs offices deal with them upon the request of the state control body in quality. The list of import goods that shall have to be examined, the list of competent authorities taking charge of state control in quality shall be stipulated in the Decision 117/1999/QD-BKHCNMT of January 26, 2000 of the Ministry of Science, Technology and Environment (now the Ministry of Science and Technology).

3. Import goods quarantine

Only items of goods included in the list of export and import goods subject to animal and vegetable quarantine which is proclaimed by the Minister of Agriculture and Rural Development, subject to aquatic-products quarantine which is proclaimed by the Minister of Aquiculture, shall have to go through quarantine procedures. Non-commercial import and export goods are not required to be quarantined, except for cases where quarantine organizations send the notifications of quarantine for each item of goods at each specific time.

Transit goods via air routes, sea routes that are not unloaded do not belong to the subjects to be quarantined.

Import goods quarantine is carried out in a mode of pre-registration and post-examination. The goods owner shall have to register for quarantine with the quarantine agencies. The quarantine agencies may perform goods quarantine at the same time when the customs offices examine the goods or after the clearance of the goods.

The goods owners compare actually imported goods with the goods included in the list of import goods subject to quarantine, which is proclaimed by the competent authority in each period, so as to determine the item of goods to be quarantined and register with the agencies in charge of quarantine for carrying out goods quarantine.

As carrying out customs procedures, apart from the customs dossiers as specified, the goods owners must submit to the customs offices the paper of quarantine registration which is confirmed by the quarantine agency.

The goods performed post-quarantine shall have to be transported and maintained the status quo till coming to the registered places. The goods shall be only put into circulation as the quarantine agencies grant the quarantine certificates.

The goods owners shall have to execute the decision by the quarantine agencies (if any) for the goods. For cases where the goods are forced to be re-exported due to insufficient conditions for being imported, the goods owners must submit the goods and the decision of the quarantine agencies and the import dossiers for carrying out procedures at the border gate.

Unit 7 Inspection, Quarantine and Checking of Goods

> **Topic discussion:**

Discuss with your partners the basic requirements and principles of inspection, quarantine and checking of goods.

其他常用词汇和短语

clause n. （合同的）条款
certificate of measurement and weight 货载衡量证书
continuous sampling 连续抽样
dispatch n. & v. 派遣
final and binding 最终并有约束力的
entry-exit inspection and quarantine bureau 进出口检验检疫局
inception of carriage 货车检查
inspect v. 检验
inspect A for B 检查 A 中是否有 B
inspection after construction 施工后检验
inspection and acceptance 验收
inspection and certificate fee 检验签证费
inspection before delivery 交货前检验
inspection between process 工序间检验
inspection certificate 检验证明
inspection certificate of health 健康检验证书
inspection certificate of origin 产地检验证书
inspection certificate of quality 质量检验证书
inspection certificate of quantity 数量检验证书
inspection certificate of value 价值检验证书
inspection certificate of weight 重量检验证书
inspection certificate on damaged cargo 验残检验证书
inspection certificate on tank 验船证书
inspection during construction 在建工程检验
inspection of commodity 商品检验
inspection of document 单证检查
inspection of loading 监装检验
inspection of fixed asset 固定资产检查
inspection of packing 包装检验
inspection of incoming merchandise 到货验收
inspection of material 材料检验
inspection of risk 被保险物价的检查
inspection of storage 监装
inspection of voucher 凭证检验
inspection on cleanliness of dry cargo hold 干货舱清洁检验
inspection on cleanliness of tank 油舱清洁检验
inspection report 检验报告

inspection tag　检查标签
inspector of tax　税务稽查员
inspector　*n*.　检验员
inspectorate general of customs　海关稽查总局
issue（a certificate）　*v*.　出具……（证明）
open-package inspection　开箱检验
reinspect　*v*.　复验
sanitary inspection certificate　卫生检验证书
reinspection　*n*.　复验
surveyor　*n*.　检验行，公证行

Unit 8

Futures Trade and Exchange Rate
期货贸易及汇率

Learning Resources

Warming-up

In finance, a futures contract is a standardized contract between two parties to buy or sell a specified asset of standardized quantity and quality at a specified future date at a price agreed today (the futures price). The contracts are traded on a futures exchange. Futures contracts are not "direct" securities like stocks, bonds, rights or warrants. They are still securities, however, though they are a type of derivative contract. The party agreeing to buy the underlying asset in the future assumes a long position, and the party agreeing to sell the asset in the future assumes a short position.

The price is determined by the instantaneous equilibrium between the forces of supply and demand among competing buy and sell orders on the exchange at the time of the purchase or sale of the contract.

In many cases, the underlying asset to a futures contract may not be traditional "commodities" at all, that is, for financial futures, the underlying asset or item can be currencies, securities or financial instruments and intangible assets or referenced items such as stock indexes and interest rates.

The future date is called the delivery date or final settlement date. The official price of the futures contract at the end of a day's trading session on the exchange is called the settlement price for that day of business on the exchange. A closely related contract is a forward contract; they differ in certain respects. Future contracts are very similar to forward contracts, except they are exchange traded and defined on standardized assets. Unlike forwards, futures typically have interim partial settlements or "true-ups" in margin requirements. For typical forwards, the net gain or loss accrued over the life of the contract is realized on the delivery date.

A futures contract gives the holder the obligation to make or take delivery under the terms of the contract, whereas an option grants the buyer the right, but not the obligation, to establish a position previously held by the seller of the option. In other words, the owner of an options contract may exercise the contract, but both parties of a "futures contract" must fulfill the contract on the settlement date. The seller delivers the underlying asset to the buyer, or, if it is a cash-settled futures contract, then cash is transferred from the futures trader who sustained a loss to the one who made a profit. To exit the commitment prior

Unit 8 Futures Trade and Exchange Rate

to the settlement date, the holder of a futures position has to offset his/her position by either selling a long position or buying back (covering) a short position, effectively closing out the futures position and its contract obligations.

Futures contracts, or simply futures, (but not future or future contract) are exchange traded derivatives. The exchange's clearing house acts as counterparty on all contracts, sets margin requirements, and crucially also provides a mechanism for settlement.

In finance, the exchange rate (also known as the foreign-exchange rate) between two currencies specifies how much one currency is worth in terms of the other. It is the value of a foreign nation's currency in terms of the home nation's currency. For example, an exchange rate of 7.8 Yuan (RMB, ¥) to the United States dollar (USD, $) means RMB 7.8 is worth the same as USD 1. The foreign exchange market is one of the largest markets in the world. By some estimates, about 3.2 trillion USD worth of currency changes hands every day.

The spot exchange rate refers to the current exchange rate. The forward exchange rate refers to an exchange rate that is quoted and traded today but for delivery and payment on a specific future date. The price of a currency depends upon supply and demands, which is affected by many factors, including relative inflation, export competitiveness, economy growth, interest-rate differentials, deficits and debt.

Dialogues

Dialogue 1 Talking about Futures

Mr. James (J) and Ms. Woolf (W) are talking about futures and Ms. Woolf learns the basic knowledge of future trading contract from Mr. James.

W: Oh, my dear James. I know almost nothing about futures. Can you help me?

J: I' am glad to answer your questions.

W: You are so helpful. What's foreign exchange futures?

J: Foreign exchange futures is just one basic type of financial futures. Foreign exchange futures or currency futures contract is an agreement to buy or sell a specified amount of a certain currency at a predetermined rate on a given future date.

W: I see. What's commodity futures?

J: The futures markets were originally set up to allow grain producers to hedge their positions in a given crop. For example, a soybean producer might have a six-month lead time between the planting of his crop and the actual harvesting and delivering to the market. The soybean producer can hedge his position by offering to sell futures contracts for the delivery soybeans. If the price of soybeans goes down, he will have to sell his crop for less than what he anticipated when he planted the soybean, but he can still make up the difference on the soybean futures contracts.

W: But if the price rises, he will lose on the futures market but gain by selling the soybean at a higher price. That means he cannot take advantage of the rising price.

J: The futures contract can protect trade itself and might incur some loss.

W: It's said that futures contract are done on the basis of margin. Is that true?

J: Margins are determined on the basis of market risk. They are normally set at 5 to 20 percent of the value of the commodity represented by the contract.

W: I guess there must be some speculators in the futures market.

J: That's right. Actually, over 90 percent of futures contracts don't involve actual delivery of commodities or securities. Very few actual items ever change hands. While profit is the motive of speculators, they provide the market with liquidity, which is essential for a market.

W: I see. Thank you for letting me know more about futures.

J: You are welcome.

 **Dialogue 2** Talk on Exchange Rate Between a Bank Staff and a Customer

Here is the dialogue between a staff member (S) of Bank of China and an Italian customer (C).

C: Hello, sir.

S: Yes, may I help you?

C: I want to change some US dollars, as I am going to be back home, Italy, next week. Would you please help me to check today's rate between the Dollar and RMB yuan?

S: Sure. It is one hundred US dollars equivalent to eight hundred and twenty-seven RMB

Unit 8　Futures Trade and Exchange Rate

yuan by the bank's selling rate today.

C: Oh, it is becoming expensive. I was told eight hundred RMB yuan more or less is enough for one hundred US dollars.

S: That's the price last month. It was changed just a few days ago.

C: The RMB is devalued a little. It is a pity. I have to pay more to buy dollars, right?

S: Yes, pity indeed. Well, I'd like to suggest you change directly into European dollar, as you are going home.

C: That is a good idea; otherwise I will pay again when I make change from dollar into European dollar.

S: Right. As the rates between free convertible currencies are always changeable, it is better for you to change directly into the currency to be used.

C: Which currency's rate is the leading one that influences the other currencies' rates?

S: Generally, we pay much attention to the change of the dollar's rate in the international market, and against that, we then adjust the RMB's rates against other currency every-day.

C: Does the RMB follow the exchange market of the world money centers?

S: No, RMB, unlike the free convertible currencies, is an unconvertible currency that can't be used abroad. So, its rate of exchange is fixed somewhat different from those of the free convertible currencies. No one can predict the value of RMB whether it is going up or down.

C: OK, I see. I think I should change today directly into European dollar.

S: OK, I'll do it for you at once.

C: Thank you for your useful help. Bye-bye.

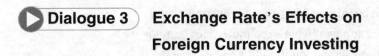

Dialogue 3　Exchange Rate's Effects on Foreign Currency Investing

Here is a dialogue between Mr. Faulkner (F) and Ms. Nora (N). They are discussing the recent foreign currency market.

F: Have you followed the value of the dollar lately?

N: How could I help but follow it? The fluctuation of dollar is killing my company! The exchange rates are eating into our profits, and we can't do anything about it.

F: It's really frustrating, isn't it? I have the same problem. I would feel a lot better if the currency was a little more stable. With the way the dollar plummeting lately, my securities have gone up in smoke.

N: Every day I have less money! I haven't spent anything, it is just melting away because of the shifts in exchange rate.

F: What we really should be making investment in is the Euro. I've followed the Euro's progress over the last quarter; I think it's about time to buy in.

N: What about the Yen?

F: Are you kidding? The Yen is in worse shape than the Dollar!

Dialogue 4 Exchange Rate's Effect on Living

Daisy (D) and Ken (K), two English tourists who are traveling in Mexico, are talking about the rapid change of the current exchange rate and its influence upon people's life.

D: You won't believe what just happened.

K: What?

D: I went down to change some money, right?

K: Yes. We need some. How much did you change?

D: I wanted to change around 500 pounds. And you know the exchange rate.

K: Yes, it's about 52 pesos for a pound, right?

D: Not today.

K: What do you mean?

D: I went into the bank with my money, and I looked at the exchange board. At first I couldn't believe it. I thought I was reading the board wrong or something.

K: Why?

D: Because the board said 102 pesos for every pound.

K: One hundred and two? That's too much. How can that be?

D: I thought it was wrong too. It didn't make sense.

K: Just two days ago it was 52. How can it be 102?

D: So, I went up to the teller and started to exchange the money. And it's true. They really gave me 102 for a pound.

K: That's amazing. How could it change so much in two days?

D: I tried to ask the bank teller why it changed, but she didn't speak English well enough. So I decided to go to the magazine shop — the one around the corner. And I bought an American newspaper.

K: What happened?

Unit 8 Futures Trade and Exchange Rate

D: It seems that yesterday the Mexican government declared it wouldn't pay back the loans it got from the World Bank. The government declared a default on the loans.

K: That's serious.

D: I know. The economy here is having serious problems. But because the government declared a default, the currency value went way down.

K: So now Mexican pesos are worth about half as much.

D: Yes, it's an amazing drop.

K: Wow. I feel sorry for the Mexicans. But it's good for us.

D: Yes, it's very good. We suddenly have twice as much money to spend here. Our hotel is now half as expensive as when we got here!

Words and Expressions

foreign exchange futures　外汇期货
financial futures　金融期货
predetermined rate　预定的汇率
commodity futures　商品期货
lead time　时间间隔
incur some loss　造成损失
margin　*n.* 保证金
speculator　*n.* 投机商
liquidity　*n.* 流动性
be equivalent to　等于，折合
devalued　*a.* （货币）贬值的

free convertible currencies　可自由兑换通货（货币）
fluctuation　波动，涨落，起伏
eat into our profits　耗掉了我们的利润
plummet　*v.* 暴跌
go up in smoke　化为乌有
melt away　逐渐消失
a default on the loans　不履行债务
currency value goes way down　币值顿时跌落

Notes

1. 期货

1) 期货的作用

期货交易是在现货交易的基础上发展起来的，通过在期货交易所买卖标准化的期货合约而进行的一种有组织的交易方式。如果将进行期货投资的人进行分类的话，大致可分为两类——套期保值者和投机者。套期保值就是对现货保值。看涨时买入（即进行多

头），在看跌时卖出期货（即空头），简单地说，就是在现货市场买进（或卖出）商品的同时，在期货市场卖出（或买入）相同数量的同种商品，进而无论现货供应市场价格怎么波动，最终都能取得在一个市场上亏损的同时在另一个市场盈利的结果，并且亏损额与盈利额大致相等，从而达到规避风险的目的。投机者则是以获取价差为最终目的，其收益直接来源于价差。投机者根据自己对期货价格走势的判断，做出买进或卖出的决定，如果这种判断与市场价格走势相同，则投机者平仓出局后可获取投机利润；如果判断与价格走势相反，则投机者平仓出局后承担投机损失。投机者主动承担风险，投机者的出现促进了市场的流动性，保障了价格发现功能的实现；对市场而言，投机者的出现缓解了市场价格可能产生的过大波动。在期货交易中套期保值者和投机者缺一不可！投机者提供套期保值者所需要的风险资金。投机者用其资金参与期货交易，承担了套期保值者所希望转嫁的价格风险。投机者的参与，使相关市场或商品的价格变化步调趋于一致，增加了市场交易量，从而增加了市场流动性，便于套期保值者对冲其合约，自由进出市场。期货的产生使投资者找到了一个相对有效的规避市场价格风险的渠道，有助于稳定国民经济，也有助于市场经济体系的建立与完善。

2）期货的分类

期货分为商品期货和金融期货。商品期货又分工业品、能源商品、农产品、其他商品等。金融期货主要是传统的金融商品（工具）如股指、利率、汇率等，各类期货交易包括期权交易等。

（1）商品期货。

① 农产品期货：如棉花、大豆、小麦、玉米、白糖、咖啡、猪腩、菜籽油、天然橡胶、棕榈油。

② 金属期货：如铜、铝、锡、锌、镍、黄金、白银。

③ 能源期货：如原油、汽油、燃料油。新兴品种包括气温、二氧化碳排放配额。

（2）金融期货。

① 股指期货：如英国 FTSE 指数、德国 DAX 指数、东京日经平均指数、香港恒生指数、沪深 300 指数。

② 利率期货。

③ 外汇期货。

2. 汇率

1）汇率与进出口

一般来说，本币汇率下降，即本币对外的币值贬低，能起到促进出口、抑制进口的作用；若本币汇率上升，即本币对外的比值上升，则有利于进口，不利于出口。

2）汇率与物价

从进口消费品和原材料来看，汇率的下降会引起进口商品在国内的价格上涨。至于它对物价总指数影响的程度则取决于进口商品和原材料在国民生产总值中所占的比重。

Unit 8 Futures Trade and Exchange Rate

反之，本币升值，其他条件不变，进口品的价格有可能降低，从而可以起到抑制物价总水平的作用。

3）汇率与资本流出入

短期资本流动常常受到汇率的较大影响。在本币对外贬值的趋势下，本国投资者和外国投资者就不愿意持有以本币计值的各种金融资产，并会将其转兑成外汇，发生资本外流现象。同时，由于纷纷转兑外汇，加剧外汇供求紧张，会促使本币汇率进一步下跌。反之，在本币对外升值的趋势下，本国投资者和外国投资者就力求持有以本币计值的各种金融资产，并引发资本内流。同时，由于外汇纷纷转兑本币，外汇供过于求，会促使本币汇率进一步上升。

1. I think I am a low risk investor.
   我想我是个低风险投资者。
2. It's the luck of the draw.
   这全靠运气。
3. The future market is very valuable to manage price risk.
   期货市场对价格风险管理很有价值。
4. Parties who have bought a future contract are said to have taken a long position.
   期货合约的购买者被认为是处在市场多头。
5. To hedge against the risk of changing prices, you'd better buy a future contract.
   为了防范价格变化所带来的风险，你最好买一份期货合约。
6. Margin requirements ensure the performance of both parties to a future contract.
   保证金要求是期货合约双方履约的保证。
7. The buying and selling of future contracts are carried out all through brokers on futures exchange.
   在期货交易所，期货合约的买卖都通过经纪商来完成。
8. The future trading market in New York is a bearish market.
   纽约的期货市场正是熊市。
9. I'd like to know the exchange rate for US Dollar.
   我想知道美元的兑换率。
10. The rate is different for different kinds of transactions.
    不同种类的交易有不同的汇率。

11. What's the rate of US dollar against RMB today?
    今天美元兑人民币的汇率是多少？
12. The exchange rate today is RMB 8.02 Yuan to USD 1.
    今天的汇率是一美元可兑 8.02 元人民币。
13. Here are the cash and exchange memo.
    这是现金和兑换水单。
14. The present rate of exchange is in our favor.
    现在的外汇率对我们有利。
15. I want to change 100 Hong Kong dollars into RMB.
    我想把 100 港元兑换成人民币。
16. Please fill out this request for foreign currency.
    请您填写外汇申请表。
17. Please tell me the currant rate for sterling.
    请告诉我英国货币的现行兑换率。
18. How many Yuan are 1,000 US dollars worth?
    1 000 美元可以兑换成多少人民币？
19. The currencies have been allowed to float, that is, their value is determined by the price bring on the open market.
    现在允许汇率浮动，即是，它的价值由它在公开市场上的价格所决定。
20. Foreign exchange rates are now free to change according to the laws of supply and demand.
    现在外汇汇率是按照供需规律自由地变化。

Exercises

I Complete the following dialogues.

1. A: _____?
   （能否告诉我人民币的现价？）
   B: Yes, the current rate for RMB is...

2. A: _____?
   （美元今天的售价是多少？）
   B: Today the dollar is going for...

Unit 8 Futures Trade and Exchange Rate

3. **A:** _____?
   （换成日本币是多少？）
   B: It will be... in Japanese currency.

4. **A:** _____.
   （请告诉我这些美元可以兑换多少钱。）
   B: If you'll wait a moment, I'll find out the rates of exchange.

5. **A:** Please tell me the current rate for sterling.
   B: _____.
   （今天的兑换率是一英镑可兑 200 日元。）

6. **A:** What kind of investor are you?
   B: _____.
   （我想我是个高风险投资者。）

7. **A:** It's said that futures contract are done on the basis of margin, is that true?
   B: _____.
   （保证金要求是期货合约双方履约的保证。）

8. **A:** How about the future trading market in New York?
   B: _____.
   （纽约的期货市场正是熊市。）

9. **A:** _____?
   （期货和期权有哪些功能？）
   B: One is hedging for keeping the value of commodities and another is to gain profit.

10. **A:** Who carry out the buying and selling of future contracts on futures exchange?
    B: _____.
    （在期货交易所，期货合约的买卖都通过经纪商来完成的。）

II Situational practice.

The situation: Mr. Li, the secretary of ABC Company, is going to sign a compensation trade contract with an American company. He is discussing with Mr. Vincent, the secretary of the American company about the exchange rate clause.

The task: Create a dialogue about the exchange rate clause.

对话汉译

对话1 讨论期货问题

詹姆斯先生（J）和伍尔夫女士（W）正讨论期货的相关问题，伍尔夫女士就期货的一些问题请教了詹姆斯先生。

W: 詹姆斯先生，我对期货几乎是一无所知。您能帮助我吗？

J: 我很乐意回答您的问题。

W: 您太好了。那什么是外汇期货呢？

J: 外汇期货是金融期货的一种基本种类。外汇期货或货币期货合约是一种协议，规定在将来的特定时间按预定的汇率买入或卖出一定金额的货币。

W: 明白了。那什么是商品期货呢？

J: 期货市场最初是为保证粮食生产者的某一种作物的价值而产生的。例如，大豆生产者播种大豆至收获后销往市场的时间间隔可能是6个月。大豆的价格在上市之前就可能会有很大的变化。大豆生产者可以通过卖出大豆期货合约来防范这种风险。如果大豆价格下跌，生产者销售大豆的价格就会低于播种大豆时的期望价格。然而，大豆期货合约可以弥补这项损失。

W: 但是如果价格上涨，他在期货市场上就会亏损，但可以以更高的价格销售大豆。也就是说，他不能得到价格上涨所带来的好处。

J: 是的，期货合约在规避商品价格变化风险的同时，也有可能造成损失。

W: 据说期货市场交易需要交纳保证金，对吧？

J: 对的。保证金是由市场风险决定的，一般是合同商品价值的5%～20%。

W: 我想期货市场上肯定有些投机商。

J: 是的。实际上，90%以上的期货交易都不涉及商品或证券的实际转让。只有极少数的实际交易发生。虽然投机商的动机就是利润，但他们赋予了市场更大的流动性。流动性是市场的根本要素。

W: 我知道了。谢谢您，詹姆斯先生，您让我对期货交易有了更多的了解。

J: 不用客气。

Unit 8 Futures Trade and Exchange Rate

▶ 对话 2　银行职员和客户讨论汇率问题

这是一位中国银行的职员（S）和一位意大利顾客（C）之间的对话。

C: 您好，先生。
S: 您好，您有什么事儿吗？
C: 我想兑换些美元，因为我下周就要回意大利去。请您帮忙查一下今天美元兑换人民币的汇率，好吗？
S: 好的。按照银行今天的美元卖出价，100 美元兑换 827 元人民币。
C: 哦，涨价了。我听说大约 800 元人民币就可以兑换 100 美元了。
S: 那是上个月的价格，就是在几天前才变更的。
C: 很遗憾，人民币有些贬值呀。我不得不花更多的人民币来换美元了，对吧？
S: 是的，的确是很遗憾。但是，既然您要回家，我建议您直接兑换成欧元。
C: 这是个好主意。否则，从美元兑换成欧元的时候，我还得再支付一笔费用。
S: 是的。由于可自由兑换货币之间的汇率总是在变动，所以您最好直接换成将要使用的货币。
C: 哪一种货币的汇率最能导致其他货币的汇率波动呢？
S: 一般情况下，我们非常重视国际市场中美元汇率的变化，并根据它的变化，我们每天调整人民币对其他货币的汇率。
C: 人民币价格是否与世界货币中心汇市挂钩呢？
S: 不挂钩。人民币和可自由兑换货币不同，它是不可自由兑换的货币，在国外不能使用。因此，人民币汇率的确定与自由兑换货币的汇率的确定有所不同。没有人可以预测人民币汇率会上升还是会下降。
C: 好，我明白了。我看我还是今天直接兑换成欧元吧。
S: 好，我马上帮您办理。
C: 非常感谢您的帮助。再见。

▶ 对话 3　汇率对外汇投资的影响

这是福克纳先生（F）和诺拉女士（N）的对话，她们讨论的话题是近期的外汇市场。

F: 最近你注意美元的价格了吗？
N: 我怎么能不关心呢？美元的价格波动快要把我们的公司搞垮了！汇率变化耗掉了我们的利润，而且我们对此毫无办法。
F: 这事真让人灰心丧气，是不是？我也遇到了同样的问题。我觉得如果货币再稍微稳定些，情况可能会好些。由于最近美元暴跌，我的有价证券已经化为灰烬。

N：我的钱一天天变少！我一分钱还没花，但这些钱因为汇率变化而逐渐消失。

F：我们真的应该把钱投在欧元上。上一季度我注意过欧元的变化，我认为现在该买进了。

N：日元怎么样？

F：你开玩笑吧？日元比美元的情况还糟糕！

对话 4　汇率对生活的影响

两位英国旅游者黛西（D）和肯（K）到墨西哥观光游览，他们在谈论汇率的急剧变化对游客生活的影响。

D：你不会相信刚刚发生了什么。

K：什么事？

D：我刚才去楼下换钱，对不对？

K：对啊，我们需要一些，你换了多少？

D：我想要换 500 左右的，而且你很清楚汇率。

K：是啊，大概是 52 比索兑换 1 英镑，对不对？

D：今天不是。

K：什么意思？

D：我带了钱去银行，然后看着汇率表。一开始，我真不敢相信，我想我读错了或什么的。

K：为什么？

D：因为汇率表上说 102 比索兑换 1 英镑。

K：102？太多了吧，怎么会这样呢？

D：我也以为错了，这样不太合理。

K：就在两天前还是 52，怎么变成 102 了呢？

D：于是我走向出纳员要求兑换钱，原来是真的。1 英镑真换了 102 比索。

K：太不可思议了！两天内怎么会改变这么多呢？

D：我试着问银行出纳员为何汇率改了，但是她的英文说得不太好。所以，我去街角那家杂志店买了一份美国报纸。

K：发生什么事了？

D：好像昨天墨西哥政府宣告不偿还向世界银行借的贷款，他们宣称不履行债务。

K：那很严重喔！

D：我知道，这儿的经济有很严重的问题，但是因为政府宣称不履行债务，币值顿时跌落。

K：所以现在墨西哥比索只值原来的一半。

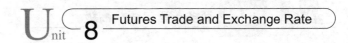

D: 是啊，真惊人的下跌。

K: 哇，我真是替墨西哥人感到遗憾，但是这种情况对我们是有利的。

D: 是啊，蛮好的，我们突然有两倍的钱来花。旅馆费现在只有刚到时的一半贵。

Extended Reading

Foreign Exchange Transactions

Today many companies will be taking a second look at their operation to make sure that their business is at its peak performance with minimum expense or overhead. Foreign exchange transaction have been largely overlooked by many businesses simply because of a lack of awareness and specialists that would be willing to help them.

Step 1

If you are using the services of foreign exchange company (most likely they would be privately held), do not fool yourself — they are in business to make money and the money they make is the money that don't end up in your bank accounts. Using an independent foreign exchange specialist/consultant will be a starting point in assessing your present situation vs. what was happening before vs. how you can make future improvements to save money.

Step 2

Definition of a broker: broker is a party that mediates between a buyer and a seller. If you deal with only one company the person on the other end of the phone is not a broker, it's a salesman that is trying to sell you foreign currency for as much as they can. Not an uncommon business practice but at the end of the day it's all about your money and it's up to you to know what you should be paying and for what. Trust is a good thing but preventing others from breaching that trust is even better.

Step 3

Ideally you will hire a foreign exchange specialist who will be able to provide you with independent assessment. Since this person will be working for you and for you only their mandate will be to protect your interest and your money.

Step 4

Providing your accounting department with regular training on handling foreign exchange transaction can be extremely effective. Many companies don't think of initially, however after realizing that they have been overpaying around $1,000 on a $100,000 monthly transaction (x12 month is $12,000 annually) they change their priority list.

Step 5

The biggest secret to a perfectly timed trade is few simple components. First, remember that this is not a gamble, you are conducting a commercial foreign exchange transaction not placing bets on the currency market. Second, you are not going to beat the market, you are going to make calculated decisions required to run your foreign currency cash flow. Third, diversify — don't just use spot trading technique, make sure you utilize and implement forwards contract (with or without options) and market orders (with or without options).

Step 6

Here is the FORMULA to help you with transaction execution: what was the exchange rate on your last transaction vs. what is that rate today vs. when you need to complete this transaction vs. market short term trends. Now, take the word "rick" out of this formula and there is your decision. It will not always be perfect, but I guarantee that 8 times out of 10 you will be right on.

Topic discussion:

How should we handle the commercial foreign exchange transactions?

其他常用词汇和短语

arbitrage *n.* 套利
asked (offer) price 卖方报价
at par 按票面价值（买卖）
at-the-money *n.* 平价期权，价内期权（也叫实值期权）
averaging *n.* 平均法，拉平价格
away *ad.* 偏离（指交易、报价偏离当前市场状况）
backing and filling 盘整
be biased bearishly 偏向熊市
bear covering 空头回补
bear market 熊市
bear raid 大量沽空
best effort 证券代销
bid market 卖方市场（买盘多于卖盘的市场）
bid *n. & v.* 买方叫价
broker *n.* 经纪人
brokerage *n.* 经纪人收取的佣金
bucket shop 非法（地下）经纪公司
bull market 牛市
buoyant *a.* 坚挺（强势上涨）的
business inventories and sales 商业库存与销售

Unit 8 Futures Trade and Exchange Rate

buy a dip   下跌时买入，逢低买入
buy in   买入平仓
buyer's market   买方市场
buyer's option   买方选择权
buying   n.   买进
call option   买入期权
call purchase   看涨买入
call sale   看跌卖出
congested market   横向市场盘整
consolidation   n.   盘整
constrain   v.   限制
construction spending   建筑支出
convergence   n.   趋同，期货合约和现货合约趋向一致
daily chart   日图
day trader   当日交易者
dealer   n.   交易商
declaration date   期权合约宣布的最后日期
delta   n.   德耳塔（期权价格与相应期权合约或金融工具价格之间的比值）
devalue   v.   （货币）贬值
discount   n.   贴现
durable goods orders   耐用消费品订单
employment report   就业报告
equivalent to   等于，折合
exercise notice   期权履约通知
exercise price   期权履约价格
expiry date   到期日
factor   n.   代理商
firm   a.   坚挺（强力支撑）的
first notice day   第一通知日

floor broker   场内经纪人
floor price   最低价
floor trader   证券交易所内的交易商
fluctuation   n.   波动
forward exchange rate   远期汇率
forward market   远期市场
forward months   合约月份
fresh option plays   新的期权买家
futures   n.   期货
gross domestic product   国内生产总值
harden   v.   坚挺
hedge   v.   套期保值
high   n.   高点
hit and bit   拍板成交
intraday   日内的，当天的
inverted market   倒挂市场
large stops   巨大的止损盘
last notice day   最后通知日
last trading day   最后交易日
life of contract   合同期限
limit price   价格波动幅度限制
liquid market   买卖易于成交的市场，高流通性市场
lock in   锁定收益
long hedge   多头套期保值
low   n.   低点
market maker   做市商
market participant   市场参与者
match   v.   冲抵
maximum/minimum price   最大/最小价格波动
notice day   通知日
offer   v.   卖方出价

official price　正式价格
omnibus account　综合账户
open contracts　未平仓合约
one cancels other (OCO)　非此即彼订单
open order　开口订单
open outcry　公开喊价
opening range　开市价幅
option　n.　期权，期货合约选择权
options committee　期权委员会
out-of-the-money option　虚值期权
outright forward exchange rate　直接远期汇率
overbuy　v.　超买
oversell　v.　超卖
position　v.　交易部位，头寸
pre-market　n.　场前交易
premium　n.　权利金，溢价，加价，升水
price　n.　定价
pricing-in　n.　按预定收盘价买进
pricing-out　n.　按预定收盘价卖出
primary market　初级市场
principal　n.　委托人
producer price index　生产者价格指数
profit taking　获利回吐
prompt date　交割日期
prompt　a.　即付的
put option　看跌期权，延卖期权，卖出期权
quotation　n.　报价
quotations committee　报价委员会
rally　v.　反弹，回升
range　n.　波幅

reaction　n.　反弹
realize　v.　变卖资产
recovery　n.　复苏
registered representative　登记代表
resistance barrier　阻力价位
ring committee　场内交易委员会
ring dealing broker　交易会员
rings (pits)　n.　交易场，交易池
rising lows　低点上升
risk aversion　风险转移
round from oversold territory　离开超卖区域
round-turn　n.　交易回合
sale down　递跌买入
scalp　n.　小投机
security deposit　保证金
sell into strength strategy　逢高卖出
selling hedge　卖出套期保值
settlement business day　结算营业日
settlement price　结算价格
short hedge　卖出套期保值
short sale　卖空
short selling　卖空
short squeeze　轧空头，逼空
short　n.　空头
spot market　现货市场
spot month　现货月
spread　n.　价差或利差
spreading　n.　套期图利
square　v.　回补
squeeze　v.　价格挤压
stall　v.　盘整
stop　n.　止损位

Unit 8 Futures Trade and Exchange Rate

stop-loss order 止损指令
straddle n. 马鞍型期权合约，套期图利
strike price 成交价
strong market 坚挺的市场
support point 支持价位
swaps n. 掉期
taker n. 购买者
target n. 目标位
tender v. 偿付
test lower 测试更低价位
the fixed-weight deflators 加权固定价格指数
the implicit deflators 隐含价格指数
thin market 成交清淡的市场
tick n. 点（期货合约的最小价格）
tight market 成交活跃的市场
time value 时间价值
trade house 经纪行
tradable amount 市场允许的最小交易量
trade house 贸易行
trend n. 趋势
turnover n. 交易量
two-way market 双向市场
unit of trading 交易单位
unload v. 抛售
underlying futures contract 期权期货合约
unofficial price 非正式价格
unwinding n. 冲底，平仓
value spot 现汇价
variation margin 价格变动保证金
volatile market 多变市场
volatility n. 易变性（年度潜在易变性）
warrant n. 仓单
weak market 疲软的市场
writer n. 期权合约中的卖方

Unit 9

Appeal, Claim and Arbitration
申诉、索赔及仲裁

Learning Resources

Warming-up

In the law, an appeal is a process for requesting a formal change to an official decision. The specific procedures for appealing, including even whether there is a right of appeal from a particular type of decision, can vary greatly from country to country. Even within a jurisdiction, the nature of an appeal can vary greatly depending on the type of case. In different jurisdictions, appellate courts are also called appeals courts, courts of appeals, superior courts, or supreme courts.

In the law, a claim (sometimes called a cause of action) is a set of facts sufficient to justify a right to sue to obtain money, property, or the enforcement of a right against another party. The phrase may refer to the legal theory upon which a plaintiff brings suit (such as breach of contract, battery, or false imprisonment). The legal document which carries a claim is often called a Statement of Claim. It can be any communication notifying the party to whom it is addressed of an alleged fault which resulted in damages from which it originates, often expressed in amount of money the receiving party should pay or reimburse.

Arbitration, a form of alternative dispute resolution (ADR), is a legal technique for the resolution of disputes outside the courts, wherein the parties to a dispute refer it to one or more persons (the "arbitrators", "arbiters" or "arbitral tribunal"), by whose decision (the "award") they agree to be bound. It is a settlement technique in which a third party reviews the case and imposes a decision that is legally binding for both sides. Other forms of ADR include mediation (a form of settlement negotiation facilitated by a neutral third party) and non-binding resolution by experts. Arbitration is a time-tested, cost-effective alternative to litigation. Hence, arbitration is most commonly used for the resolution of commercial disputes, particularly in the context of international commercial transactions.

Unit 9 Appeal, Claim and Arbitration

Dialogues

Dialogue 1 Talking about Claim

Mr. Brown (B) is discussing the claim of damaged arbutus with Ms. Wang (W), and finally it is settled amicably.

W: Hello, Mr. Brown, how are you? It is nice to see you again.

B: How are you, Ms. Wang. It certainly is a pleasure to see you again here. I hope you had an enjoyable trip from London.

W: The flight was really long, but it was comfortable, so I do not feel very tired.

B: I am glad that you had a pleasant trip. I hope you are comfortably settled and find things at the hotel satisfactory.

W: Everything is perfect, thank you. Well, now, Mr. Brown, if you don't mind, I'll get to the point.

B: OK. You want to take up the subject of the arbutus, don't you?

W: That's right. You see, Mr. Brown, you have probably been advised of the serious damage done to the last consignment of 60 cases of arbutus. Upon its arrival in London on board the S.S. Cornea, it was found, much to our regret that about 50% of the cases were leaking. Closer inspection by the Health Officers showed that the contents were considered unfit for human consumption.

B: Just a minute, if you please, Ms. Wang. Have your people in London discovered what were the exact causes of the leakage? It was rather a singular case, for thousands of tons of this product have been exported and this seems to be the only case of a shipment being damaged en route.

W: I am sorry I have to say it was not en route. It was definitely damaged prior to loading onto the S.S. Cornea. You may think it a singular case, yet the fact remains that this has made it necessary for us to file a claim on you. Here, Mr. Brown, I have brought along with me the certificate issued by the London Health Office. It speaks for itself. As to the causes, closer inspection and examination by our cargo-handling people revealed that the leakage of juice was brought about by damaged tins. They were evidently broken through careless handling while being loaded onto the ship's hold in Sydney dock.

B: As I have said before, the whole business is most unfortunate. We have never come across such a case of damage during loading.

W: I have to remind you that our terms are CIF port of London. While we have full confidence in your Commodities Inspection Bureau, this is a case that occurred after their sampling and analysis at the factory. And the broken tins through careless handling and deterioration of the contents en route brought about this state of affairs. Now, Mr. Brown, you are well aware that our business has just started this branch of activities and the loss thus sustained will be a blow to this department. I am sure you will think it fair on our part when we suggest that the total value of the parcel should be reduced by 50% and that you should give us an allowance by way of credit for the amount to be set against our future purchases of canned fruits from you.

B: To be fair to your company, I am directed by my Sydney branch to settle this issue with you amicably on the condition that you give us a certificate issued by your Health Department. Now that this is available, I think everything will be in order.

W: I am so glad to hear of your ready agreement. Your fairness in business dealing is unsurpassed. Shall we send you a letter confirming this?

B: As soon as you send us a letter confirming this conversation, we'll send you a reply immediately.

W: Thanks ever so much for your cooperation, Mr. Brown. Goodbye.

B: Goodbye.

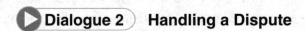

Dialogue 2 Handling a Dispute

A customer (C) discusses an error in her order with the manufacturer (M).

C: We have a problem, sir.

M: What has happened?

C: You remember that we ordered 50 of your BD-205 laser jet printers?

M: Of course. We shipped them two weeks ago. Haven't they arrived?

C: That's the problem. They've arrived, and they're the wrong model. You sent the QR-224 model. That model is not in compatible with our computer system.

M: I'm sorry to hear that. I'll look into it and try to get it corrected for you as quickly as possible. Do you have the invoice number?

C: I have a fax of the invoice right here.

M: Yes, there certainly seems to be a mistake. For some reason, we shipped the wrong model. Would you mind waiting a few minutes while I check with our shipping department?

Unit 9 Appeal, Claim and Arbitration

C: I'm anxious to get this straightened out.

M: Well, I've discovered the source of the error. It seems your customer account number was incorrectly entered into our computer at the warehouse. This resulted in the wrong shipment.

C: That's an understandable, but regrettable mistake.

M: We'll airfreight the correct printers immediately. And since it's our error, we'll pay the freight charges.

C: That's good of you. My home office will be glad to hear it.

M: I'm very pleased we were able to get to the bottom of this so quickly. Just return the wrong printers sea-freight, and our company will pick up those charges too.

C: Thank you so much.

M: That's all right. We hope to provide you with good service for many years to come.

Dialogue 3 Talking about Arbitration

Mr. Conner (C), an English businessman, is discussing with Ms. Yun (Y) the arbitration in China.

Y: Let's talk about arbitration, shall we?

C: OK. Must the arbitration be done only in China?

Y: No. Arbitration can be conducted either in China or in other countries.

C: Then, I want to know more about arbitration in China to decide whether arbitration will be held there.

Y: I see. I can tell you the details.

C: Is the cost very high?

Y: No. If you submit your dispute to arbitration, you only need to pay a reasonable fee to the China International Economic and Trade Arbitration Commission according to the Arbitration Fee Schedule.

C: What if one party does not follow the award?

Y: If things like that happen, the People's Court in China can enforce it at the request of the other party. But disputes are usually settled by friendly negotiation between the two parties.

C: I see. Thanks for your help.

Dialogue 4 Talking about Claim

Mr. Raymond (R) is requesting Mr. Walter (W) to make up his losses according to the relevant provisions under their contract.

R: Hello, Mr. Walter. There is something wrong with the goods. We have just received a consignment of peanuts from your company. I must complain about the quality of the goods.

W: What's wrong with this batch of peanuts?

R: Some of them smell musty, and some packages are damaged.

W: I have to check with the transporter.

R: I will appreciate your looking into this matter, and giving us reply within the next five days.

W: I really apologize for the inconvenience which has been caused.

R: We reserve the right to claim compensation from you for any damage.

Words and Expressions

get to the point　进入正题
take up　拿起，抱起
consignment　*n.*　托运物
closer inspection　严格检验
be unfit for　不适于
en route　在途中
prior to　在……以前
cargo-handling people　货物装卸工人
in compatible with　与……相容
look into　调查（查找）
invoice number　发票号
airfreight　*n.*　空运运费
seafreight　*n.*　海运运费
submit dispute　提交争议申请
reasonable fee　合理的费用
China International Economic and Trade Arbitration Commission　中国国际经济贸易仲裁委员会
follow the award　执行决议
enforce　*v.*　强制实施

Unit 9 Appeal, Claim and Arbitration

1. 商业活动索赔

在执行合同的过程中，签约双方都应该严格履行合同义务。任何一方如果不能严格履行，就会给另一方带来麻烦。在这种情况下，受损失的一方有权根据合同规定要求责任方赔偿损失或采取其他补救措施。受损失的一方采取的这种行动称之为"索赔"，而责任方就受损失一方提出的要求进行处理，叫作"理赔"。在业务中常见的是买方向卖方提出索赔，如卖方拒不交货、逾期装运、数量短缺、货物的品质规格与合同不符、错发错运、包装不妥、随船单证不全或漏填错发等致使买方遭受损失时，买方可向卖方提出索赔。但是在某些情况下，卖方也向买方提出索赔要求，如买方拒开或迟开信用证、不按时派船、无理毁约等致使卖方遭受损失时，卖方也会向买方提出索赔。

2. 仲裁的基本程序

为了确保仲裁裁决的公正及时，仲裁必须依法定程序进行。仲裁的法定程序主要分为4个阶段。

（1）受理阶段。仲裁程序是以当事人向仲裁机构申请仲裁为起始。仲裁委员会收到当事人提交的仲裁申请书后，认为符合受理条件的，在收到仲裁申请书之日起五日内向申请人发出受理通知书，同时向被申请人发出仲裁通知书及附件。双方当事人在收到受理通知书或仲裁通知书后，应当做好以下几项工作：申请人须在规定的期限内预交仲裁费用，否则将视为申请人撤回仲裁申请；被申请人可在仲裁通知书规定的期限内向仲裁委员会提交书面答辩书；分别做好证据材料的核对及整理工作，必要时可提交补充证据；及时提交仲裁员选定书、法定代表人证明书、详细写明委托权限的授权委托书等有关材料；在被申请人下落不明的情况下，申请人应主动查找其下落，并向仲裁委员会提交被申请人的确切住所，否则将影响仲裁程序进行；被申请人若要提出仲裁反请求，则必须在仲裁规则规定的期限内提出。此外，双方当事人均有权向仲裁委员会申请财产保全和证据保全，有权委托律师和其他代理人进行仲裁活动。

（2）组庭阶段。双方当事人应当在规定的期限内约定仲裁庭的组成方式和选定仲裁员。若当事人在规定的期限内未能约定仲裁庭的组成方式或者选定仲裁员的，由仲裁委员会主任指定。仲裁庭组成后，仲裁委员会向双方当事人发出组庭通知书。当事人在收到组庭通知书后，对仲裁员的公正性有怀疑时，可以在首次开庭前提出回避申请，同时应当说明理由。若回避事由在首次开庭后知道的，可以在最后一次开庭终结前提出。因回避而重新选定或指定仲裁员后，当事人可以请求已进行的仲裁程序重新进行，是否准许，由仲裁庭决定。

（3）开庭审理阶段。仲裁委员会应当在仲裁规则规定的期限内将开庭日期通知双方当事人。当事人在收到开庭通知书后，应当注意以下几个问题。

① 当事人若确有困难，不能在所定的开庭日期到庭，则可以在仲裁规则规定的期限内向仲裁庭提出延期开庭请求，是否准许，由仲裁庭决定。申请人经书面通知，无正当理由不到庭或未经仲裁庭许可中途退庭的，视为撤回仲裁申请。被申请人经书面通知，无正当理由不到庭或者未经仲裁庭许可中途退庭的，仲裁庭可以缺席裁决。

② 在庭审过程中，当事人享有进行辩论和表述最后意见的权利。

③ 双方当事人应当严格遵守开庭纪律。

④ 当事人申请仲裁后，有自行和解的权利。达成和解协议的，可以请求仲裁庭根据和解协议做出裁决，也可撤回仲裁申请。在庭审过程中，若双方当事人自愿调解的，可在仲裁庭主持下先行调解。调解成功的，仲裁庭依据已达成的调解协议书制作调解书，当事人可以要求仲裁庭根据调解协议制作裁决书。调解不成的，则由仲裁庭及时做出裁决。仲裁庭对专门性问题认为需要鉴定的，可以交由当事人共同约定的鉴定部门鉴定，也可以由仲裁庭指定的鉴定部门鉴定，鉴定费用由当事人预交。

（4）裁决阶段。仲裁庭在将争议事实调查清楚、宣布闭庭后，应进行仲裁庭评议，并按照评议中的多数仲裁员的意见做出裁决。若仲裁庭不能形成多数意见时，则按照首席仲裁员的意见做出裁决。在裁决阶段，双方当事人享有以下几项权利。

① 有权根据实际情况，要求仲裁庭就事实已经清楚的部分先行裁决。

② 在收到裁决书后的三十日内，当事人有权对裁决书中的文字、计算错误或者遗漏的事项申请仲裁庭补正。

③ 双方当事人在收到裁决书后，应当自觉履行仲裁裁决。

1. Generally a party has the right to appeal any judgment to at least one higher court.
   通常当事人对任何判决拥有至少一次上诉权。
2. Costs will be shared equally between the two parties.
   诉讼费由双方当事人平均分担。
3. Defendants successfully obtained the dismissal of an appeal but were awarded no costs.
   被告成功地让法院驳回了上诉，但却没得任何诉讼费。
4. Claims occur frequently in international trade.
   国际贸易中经常发生索赔现象。
5. I've heard that you have lodged a claim against us.
   听说你们已经向我们提出了索赔。

Unit 9 Appeal, Claim and Arbitration

6. We filed a claim with (against) you for the short weight.
   关于短重问题，我们已经向你方提出索赔。

7. We lodged a claim with you on grape wine yesterday.
   昨天我们就葡萄酒问题向贵方提出索赔。

8. We are not in a position to entertain your claim.
   我们不能接受你们提出的索赔要求。

9. We are now lodging a claim with you.
   我们现在向贵方提出索赔。

10. We have received the letters giving full details of this claim.
    我们已经收到了内容详尽的索赔信件。

11. We have received your remittance in settlement of our claim.
    我们已经收到你方解决我们索赔问题的汇款。

12. We may consider withdrawing the claim.
    我们可以考虑撤回索赔要求。

13. We should settle the dispute through negotiations without resorting to legal proceeding.
    我们应该通过仲裁解决争议而非法律途径。

14. Where do you want to have arbitration held?
    你想在什么地方进行仲裁？

15. All disputes in connection with this contract shall be settled through friendly negotiation.
    所有有关合同的争议应友好商议。

16. At the hearing, the arbitrators ask questions and try to get as much information regarding the facts concerning the truth.
    在听证会上，仲裁人提问并尽可能多地获得有关案件事实的情况。

17. Generally speaking, all the fees for arbitration shall be borne by the losing party unless otherwise awarded by the court.
    一般来讲，所有的仲裁费用由败诉方买单，除非法院另有判决。

18. The decision made by the arbitration commission shall be accepted as final and binding upon both parties.
    仲裁委员会做出的决定应为最终裁决并对双方具有约束力。

19. If you are not prepared to compensate our loss, we suggest that case be submitted for arbitration.
    若你们不赔偿我方损失，我们建议提交仲裁。

20. We are now applying formally to the arbitration commission for arbitration of this dispute.
    我们现在正式向仲裁委员会就此争议申请仲裁。

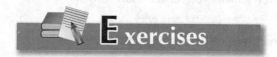

I **Complete the following dialogues.**

1. **A:** _____.
   （发现五箱破损，里面的装置严重损坏。）
   B: Really! That's something unexpected.

2. **A:** The goods were in perfect condition when they left here.
   B: _____.
   （我们的调查报告显示，损坏是由于包装不当引起的。）

3. **A:** _____.
   （请尽最大努力圆满解决此事。）
   B: We'll get in touch with the shipping company and see what can be done.

4. **A:** Was the damage extensive?
   B: _____.
   （我看大概有一半的货不能用了。）

5. **A:** _____.
   （你的赔偿问题终于解决了。）
   B: Thanks, we appreciate the fast work.

6. **A:** _____.
   （我们会向货运公司着手申请赔偿的。）
   B: We'll wait and see what they say.

7. **A:** Just whose fault is this damage?
   B: _____.
   （货离开工厂时都是完好无缺的啊。）

8. **A:** _____.
   （抱歉，不过我不认为这次的损坏是我们的错。）
   B: What do you mean?

9. **A:** Though everything may be as you say, there are many factors involved. _____
   _____.
   （况且，你方检验员并没有提及造成损坏的任何原因。）
   B: The mushrooms were packed in small one pound plastic bags, sixty of these bags to a carton. It is stated on the surveyors' report that external conditions of goods at the time of survey are all sound and intact. So obviously the cause of the damage is that the

Unit 9 Appeal, Claim and Arbitration

mushrooms were not completely dried before packing

10. **A:** As you know, before shipment, the Commodity Inspection Bureau inspected the goods in question. They concluded that the goods were well dehydrated from fresh and choice material and up to standard for export.

    B: I think the Inspection Bureau at your end, when effecting inspection, only selected a few package at random—these happened to be up to the standard. _____.
    （由于波及的数量只是整批货的 20%，我想你方应该赔偿。）

II Situational practice.

The situation: You and Mr. Miller negotiate the place for arbitration. You suggest arbitration will be conducted in China, while Mr. Miller insists on arbitration should be conducted in a third country.

The task: Find a partner to do role-playing.

对话汉译

对话 1　讨论索赔事宜

布朗先生（B）和王女士（W）正在讨论杨梅受损赔付一事，并通过友好协商解决了该问题。

W: 布朗先生，你好。很高兴再次见到你。
B: 王女士，你好。很荣幸在这里又见到你。希望你从伦敦来一路旅途愉快。
W: 飞行时间虽长，但客机非常舒适，所以也不觉得很累。
B: 我很高兴你旅途愉快。希望你住得舒适，旅馆设备都还觉得满意。
W: 谢谢你，一切都很好。噢，布朗先生，要是你不介意的话，现在咱们就步入正题吧。
B: 好，你想谈谈杨梅的事，对不对？
W: 对。布朗先生，也许你已经知道最后一批 60 箱的杨梅严重损坏的情况了。"柯娜"轮一到达伦敦的时候，我们就遗憾地发现其中有一半左右的箱子渗漏。经卫生检疫局官员仔细检查，认为内装食品不可供人们食用。
B: 王女士，请稍等。请问伦敦的人有没有发现渗漏的确切原因？这件事还只有这么一次，我们已经出口好几千吨了，在中途损坏还是头一回。

W: 很抱歉，我得说明，损坏不是在运输途中发生的。很明显，损坏是在装上"柯娜"轮号前发生的。你可能认为这事是头一回，可事实不得不让我们向你们提出索赔。布朗先生，这是伦敦卫生检疫局官员签发的证明，上面写得一清二楚。至于原因，经过我们负责装卸的人仔细检查，结果发现果汁渗漏的原因是锡罐被损坏了。很明显是在悉尼码头装船时，因搬运疏忽大意而造成锡罐受损。

B: 我刚才讲过，整件事实在是很不幸。我们从未遇到过罐头在装船时发生这样的损坏。

W: 我不得不提醒你，我们的条款是伦敦到岸价。虽然我们很信赖你们的商品检验局，可是损坏是在工厂抽样化验之后发生的，是由于搬运不慎而锡罐破裂，中途食品变质所造成的。布朗先生，你很清楚我们才开始经营这项业务，蒙受的损失将对业务部门是一个打击。我们建议这批货从总价中削减百分之五十，并给予我们补贴，这些款项就用于将来向你们订购罐头水果时冲销，我相信你认为这样对我们才是公平的。

B: 悉尼分公司派我来和你们公平友好地解决这件事，前提条件就是把你们卫生部签发的证明给我们。现在证明已经有了，我想事情都会顺利解决的。

W: 听到你这么欣然地同意了，我很高兴。办理业务这么公平，真是无法比啊。我们将寄信让你们确认好吗？

B: 我们一旦收到你们的来信确认此次谈话，就会立即回复。

W: 万分感谢你的合作。布朗先生，再见。

B: 再见。

对话 2　处理争议问题

一位顾客（C）正与生产商（M）协调发货出错的问题。

C: 我们有一个问题，先生。

M: 发生了什么事？

C: 你还记得我们订购贵公司 50 台 BD205 激光打印机吗？

M: 当然。我们两周前已经发货。货到了吗？

C: 这就是问题所在。货已经到了，但型号错了，贵公司发送的是 QR 224 型。这一款与我们的电脑系统不兼容。

M: 真遗憾。我会进行核查并纠正问题。你有发票号码吗？

C: 我这里有一份传真发票。

M: 是的，我们发错货了。请等待几分钟，我与我们的航运部门联系核实，好吗？

C: 我希望尽快解决问题。

M: 我已经找到了错误的原因了。仓库电脑上您的客户账号输错了，这导致了发货错误。

Unit 9 Appeal, Claim and Arbitration

C: 可以理解，但也深表遗憾。
M: 我们将立即空运型号正确的打印机。由于这是我们的错误，我们将支付运费。
C: 你们的服务真不错，我们很欣慰。
M: 我很高兴能这么快解决问题。请将已收到的打印机海运回我公司，我们将承担返回打印机的海运费。
C: 谢谢您。
M: 不客气。我们希望为您提供长期良好的服务。

对话 3 讨论仲裁问题

来自英国的商人康纳先生（C）与云女士（Y）正在讨论中国的仲裁问题。

Y: 我们来讨论一下仲裁问题，好吗？
C: 好的。仲裁只能在中国进行吗？
Y: 不，可以在中国进行，也可以在其他国家进行。
C: 那么我想先多了解一下中国的仲裁情况，以便决定是否在中国进行仲裁。
Y: 那好，我为您详细介绍。
C: 中国的仲裁费用很高吗？
Y: 不高。如果您要对争议进行仲裁的话，您只需要根据仲裁费用表的规定向中国国际经贸仲裁委员会缴纳合理的费用。
C: 如果有一方不执行仲裁的判决怎么办？
Y: 如果出了那种情况，中国人民法院可以根据另一方的要求强制执行。但是争议通常是通过双方的友好协商加以解决的。
C: 我明白了，谢谢您的帮助。

对话 4 讨论索赔事宜

雷蒙德先生要（R）求沃尔特先生（W）就合同所规定的条款赔偿损失。

R: 您好。沃尔特先生。我们刚收到贵公司发出的一批花生，但货品出了质量问题。
W: 什么问题呢？
R: 一些花生闻起来有股霉味，还有些外包装已经被损坏了。
W: 我会向运输公司核实。
R: 希望您对此进行调查，并在五天之内给出答复。
W: 给贵方带来的不便，我深表歉意。
R: 对于您方造成的损失，我方保留索赔的权利。

Extended Reading

Arbitration Agreements

Arbitration agreements refer to written agreements between parties under which the parties are willing to submit any dispute, controversy or claim arising out of or in connection with the contract to an arbitration institution for resolution. Firstly, an agreement must be reached between the two parties on solving the disputes through arbitration. The agreement may be reached before or after the occurrence of the disputes, that is, by signing a written arbitration agreement between the interested parties. When applying for arbitration, the party concerned must submit the contract which includes a clause for arbitration or a temporary agreement on arbitration, otherwise the application will be rejected. Secondly, the ruling of arbitration is in general final. That is, the arbitrators to whom the two parties have agreed to resort shall make the final award. The interested parties cannot refuse the ruling or appeal to the court unless they can prove with fact that the arbitration is against the law or the arbitrators have acted unfairly.

There are two types of written arbitration agreements: one is arbitration clause which is concluded before the disputes arise, in which the two parties declare that in case of disputes, they are willing to submit to arbitration. This type of agreement is generally included in the contract. The other is called submission, which is concluded after the disputes arise, in which the two parties declare that they are willing to submit to arbitration. This type of arbitration agreement is independent of the contract.

Topic discussion:

Briefly explain the types of arbitration agreements.

appellant   *n.* 上诉人   appellee   *n.*   被上诉人
appellate court/court of appeal   上诉法院   arbitration agreement   仲裁协议

Unit 9 Appeal, Claim and Arbitration

arbitration association 仲裁协会
arbitration board 仲裁庭
arbitration clause 仲裁条款
arbitrator n. 仲裁员
attribute to 把……归因于
award n. 仲裁裁决
bug n. 虫子
bring up a (one's) claim 提出索赔
claim against carrier 向承运人索赔
claim for compensation 要求补偿
claim for damage 由于损坏而索赔
claim for indemnity 要求索赔
claim for inferior quality 因质量低劣而索赔
claim for loss and damage of cargo 货物损失索赔
claim for short weight 因短重而索赔
claim for trade dispute 贸易纠纷（引起的）索赔
claim letter 索赔书
claim on the goods 对某（批）货索赔
claim on 向某人（方）提出索赔
claim report 索赔报告
claim n. & v. 索赔，赔偿；赔偿金
claimant n. 索赔人
claimee n. 被索赔人
claiming administration 索赔局
claims assessor 估损人
claims department/commission 索赔委员会
claims documents 索赔证件
claims rejected 拒赔
claims settlement 理赔

claims settling agent 理赔代理人
claims settling fee 理赔代理费
claims statement 索赔清单
claims surveying agent 理赔检验代理人
claims n. 索赔，债权
claimsman n. 损失赔偿结算人
compensate v. 赔偿，补偿
compensation n. 赔偿金
consequence n. 结果，后果
contamination n. 污染，弄脏
dehydrate v. 脱水，干燥
file a (one's) claim 提出索赔
impartial a. 公正的
improper a. 不合适的
in settlement of 解决
in the amount of 金额为……
inability n. 无能力
incorrect a. 不正确的
incur v. 遭受，带来
insurance claim 保险索赔
liability n. 责任，义务
lodge a (one's) claim 提出索赔
make a (one's) claim 提出索赔
make a claim for (on) sth. 就某事提出索赔
make a claim with (against) sb. 向某人（方）提出索赔
make an investigation 调查研究
mishap n. 不幸事故，灾难
mouldy a. 发霉的，陈腐的
oversight n. 疏忽，出错
precaution n. 预防，警惕，谨慎

put in a (one's) claim 提出索赔	testimony n. 证言，证词
raise a (one's) claim 提出索赔	umpire n. 仲裁员
register a (one's) claim 提出索赔	unmerchantable a. 不适于出售的
reveal v. 揭示	unsurpassed a. 无比的，卓越的
sales confirmation 销售确认书	voyage n. 航程，航行
settle a claim 解决索赔（问题）	waive v. 放弃，撤回
singular a. 独一无二的，独个的	waive a claim 放弃索赔（要求）
submit for arbitration 提交仲裁	withdraw a claim 撤销（某项）索赔

Appendix A Glossary
词 汇 表

Words
单 词

accessory   *n.*   附件，配饰
accommodation   *n.*   通融
airfreight   *n.*   空运运费
amendment   *n.*   改正，修改
appellant   *n.*   上诉人
appellee   *n.*   被上诉人
arbitrage   *n.*   套利
arbitration   *n.*   仲裁
arbitrator   *n.*   仲裁员
at-the-money   *n.*   平价期权，价内期权（也叫实值期权）
authorize   *v.*   授权，批准
available   *a.*   可得到的
averaging   *n.*   平均法，拉平价格
award   *n.*   仲裁裁决
away   *ad.*   偏离（指交易、报价偏离当前市场状况）
backlog   *n.*   待办事项
bag/sack   *n.*   袋
bargain   *v.*   讨价还价
barrel   *n.*   琵琶桶，粗腰桶
basket   *n.*   篮，篓，筐
bid   *n.* & *v.*   买方叫价
bottle   *n.*   瓶

box   *n.*   盒
breakage   *n.*   破损（险）
broker   *n.*   经纪人
brokerage   *n.*   经纪人收取的佣金
bug   *n.*   虫子
bundle   *n.*   捆，束
buoyant   *a.*   坚挺（强势上涨）的
buying   *n.*   买进
can/tin   *n.*   罐，听
canvas   *n.*   帆布
carton   *n.*   纸板箱，纸箱
case/chest   *n.*   箱
cask   *n.*   桶
casket   *n.*   小箱
cellophane   *n.*   玻璃纸
chest   *n.*   箱
claim   *n.* & *v.*   索赔，赔偿；赔偿金
claimant   *n.*   索赔人
claimee   *n.*   被索赔人
claims   *n.*   索赔，债权
claimsman   *n.*   损失赔偿结算人
clarify   *v.*   讲清楚，澄清
clause   *n.*   （合同的）条款
clerical   *a.*   记录的

coil　　　　n.　捆，卷
compensate　　v.　赔偿，补偿
compensation　n.　赔偿金
concession　　n.　让步
consequence　　n.　结果，后果
consignee　　n.　收货人
consigner　　n.　发货人
consignment　n.　托运物
consolidation　n.　盘整
constrain　　v.　限制
container　　n.　集装箱
contamination　n.　污染，弄脏
contract　　n.　合同
contractor　　n.　订约人，承包人
convergence　n.　趋同，期货合约和现货合约趋向一致
corrosive　　n.　腐蚀性物品
coverage　　n.　（保险合同所列的）险别
crate　　n.　板条箱
customs　　n.　海关，关税
cylinder　　n.　铁桶，汽缸
dealer　　n.　交易商
dehydrate　　v.　脱水，干燥
delivery　　n.　交货
delta　　n.　德耳塔（期权价格与相应期权合约或金融工具价格之间的比值）
demurrage　　n.　滞期费
devalue　　v.　（货币）贬值
devalued　　a.　（货币）贬值的
discount　　n.　贴现
dispatch　　n.& v.　派遣
dispatch　　v.　派遣
disqualification　n.　质量不合格
divide　　v.　分割，区分
drum　　n.　圆桶

duration　　n.　持续时间，为期
enforce　　v.　强制实施
expedite　　v.　加快（进程等）
explosive　　n.　爆炸品
factor　　n.　代理商
fireworks　　n.　礼花
firm　　a.　坚挺（强力支撑）的
florin（guilder）n.　荷兰盾
fluctuation　n.　波动
formality　　n.　正式手续
fragile　　n.　易碎品
freshwater　　n.　淡水（险）
futures　　n.　期货
harden　　v.　坚挺
hedge　　v.　套期保值
high　　n.　高点
hogshead　　n.　大桶
impartial　　a.　公正的
improper　　a.　不合适的
inability　　n.　无能力
incorrect　　a.　不正确的
incur　　v.　遭受，带来
inflammable　n.　易燃物
inspect　　v.　检验
inspector　　n.　检验员
insure　　v.　为……投保
intact　　a.　完整的，未损伤的
irrevocable　　a.　不可撤销的
issue（a certificate）　v.　出具……（证明）
keg　　n.　小桶
layout　　n.　布局，安排，设计
leakage　　n.　漏损（险）
liability　　n.　责任，义务
liner　　n.　定期轮船，班轮

Appendix A Glossary

liquidity *n.* 流动性
loophole *n.* 漏洞
low *n.* 低点
margin *n.* 保证金
mark *n.* 标志，噱头
match *v.* 冲抵
mishap *n.* 不幸事故，灾难
mouldy *a.* 发霉的，陈腐的
offer *n.* 出价
    v. 卖方出价
option *n.* 期权，期货合约选择权
order *n.* 订单，订购
Osaka *n.* 大阪（日本地名）
overbuy *v.* 超买
oversell *v.* 超卖
oversight *n.* 疏忽，出错
package *n.* 包装（指包、捆、束、箱等），包裹
packet *n.* 小包
packing *n.* 包装（法）
pallet *n.* 托盘
parcel *n.* 小包，一批货
pilferage *n.* （小量地）偷
plummet *v.* 暴跌
poison *n.* 毒剂
polythene *n.* 聚乙烯
position *v.* 交易部位，头寸
precaution *n.* 预防，警惕，谨慎
pre-market *n.* 场前交易
premium *n.* 权利金，溢价，加价，升水
prestige *n.* 声誉
price *n.* 定价
priced *a.* 已标价的，已定价的
pricing *n.* 定价，标价
pricing-in *n.* 按预定收盘价买进

pricing-out *n.* 按预定收盘价卖出
principal *n.* 委托人
prompt *a.* 即付的
provision *n.* 条款
quota *n.* 配额，限额
quotation *n.* 报价
quote *v.* 报价
rally *v.* 反弹，回升
range *n.* 波幅
reaction *n.* 反弹
realize *v.* 变卖资产
recovery *n.* 复苏
reinspect *v.* 复验
reinspection *n.* 复验
retailer *n.* 零售店，零售商
reveal *v.* 揭示
rings (pits) *n.* 交易场，交易池
round-turn *n.* 交易回合
sample *n.* 样品
scalp *n.* 小投机
seafreight *n.* 海运运费
season *n.* 季节，旺季
settle *v.* 决定
short *n.* 空头
sign *v.* 签字
singular *a.* 独一无二的，独个的
speculator *n.* 投机者
spread *n.* 价差或利差
spreading *n.* 套期图利
square *v.* 回补
squeeze *v.* 价格挤压
stall *v.* 盘整
stop *n.* 止损位
straddle *n.* 马鞍型期权合约，套期图利
substantial *a.* 充实的，大量的**

surveyor n. 检验行，公证行
swaps n. 掉期
taker n. 购买者
target n. 目标位
tender v. 偿付
territory n. 代理区域
testimony n. 证言，证词
tick n. 点（期货合约的最小价格）
tramp n. 非定期轮船
transaction n. 交易，买卖
transportation n. 运输
transship v. 转运，换船
transshipment n. 转运，转船
trend n. 趋势

turnover n. 交易量
umpire n. 仲裁员
unload v. 抛售
unmerchantable a. 不适于出售的
unsurpassed a. 无比的，卓越的
unwinding n. 冲底，平仓
volatility n. 易变性（年度潜在易变性）
volume n. 量，数量
voyage n. 航程，航行
waive v. 放弃，撤回
warrant n. 仓单
workable a. 行得通的
writer n. 期权合约中的卖方

Expressions
短　　语

a batch of 一批
a default on the loans 不履行债务
abide by 遵守
abide by the contract 遵守合同
accept an order 接受订单
acknowledgement of order 订单确认
additional charge/fee 额外费用
agreement to pay 支付协议
air waybill 空运单
airway bill 航空运单
along the lines of sth./along those lines 同一类的东西
alter the contract 修改合同
annul the contract 废除合同
appellate court/court of appeal 上诉法院

apply to 向……申请（要求）
approve the contract 审批合同
arbitration agreement 仲裁协议
arbitration association 仲裁协会
arbitration board 仲裁庭
arbitration clause 仲裁条款
as is stated before 如前所述
asked (offer) price 卖方报价
associated company 联号，联营公司
at par 按票面价值（买卖）
at your end/on your side 在你方
attribute to 把……归因于
Australian dollar 澳大利亚元
Austrian schilling 奥地利先令
average price 平均价格

Appendix A Glossary 词汇表

bill of lading (B/L) 提单
back order 尚未执行的订单
backing and filling 盘整
bank bill 银行汇票
bank money 银行票据，银行货币
banker's draft 银行汇票
base price 底价
be attached to 附加于
be biased bearishly 偏向熊市
be entitled to 有权做……
be equivalent to 等于，折合
be in bad order 破损，（包装）不合格
be in good order 完好
be laid down in the contract 在合同中列明
be legally binding 受法律约束
be likely to 可能
be stipulated in the contract 在合同中予以规定
be unfit for 不适于
bear covering 空头回补
bear market 熊市
bear raid 大量沽空
bedrock price 最低价
Belgian franc 比利时法郎
best effort 证券代销
bid market 卖方市场（买盘多于卖盘的市场）
bill of exchange 汇票
bill of lading copy 副本提单
blanket order 总订单
book shipping space 订舱位
booking request 订舱申请
bottom price 最低价
breach of contract 违反合同

break the contract 毁约
bring the contract into effect 使合同生效
bring up a (one's) claim 提出索赔
bucket shop 非法（地下）经纪公司
bull market 牛市
business inventories and sales 商业库存与销售
business relations 业务关系
buy a dip 下跌时买入，逢低买入
buy in 买入平仓
buyer's market 买方市场
buyer's option 买方选择权
buying price 买价
call option 买入期权
call purchase 看涨买入
call sale 看跌卖出
Canadian dollar 加拿大元
cancel an order 撤销订单
cancel the contract 撤销合同
cancellation of contract 撤销合同
cannot commit ourselves... 我们不能保证……，我们无法承诺……
cargo receipt 货物收据
cargo-handling people 货物装卸工人
carry out 执行
carry out the contract 执行合同
cease to be in effect/force 失效
ceiling price 最高价，顶价
certificate of analysis 分析证书
certificate of conformity 一致性证书
certificate of measurement and weight 货载衡量证书
certificate of quality 质量证书
certificate of registry 船舶登记证书
charge a ship 租船

charter party 租船契约，租船人（团体）
China International Economic and Trade Arbitration Commission 中国国际经济贸易仲裁委员会
cost, insurance and freight (CIF) 到岸价格
claim against carrier 向承运人索赔
claim for compensation 要求补偿
claim for damage 由于损坏而索赔
claim for indemnity 要求索赔
claim for inferior quality 因质量低劣而索赔
claim for loss and damage of cargo 货物损失索赔
claim for short weight 因短重而索赔
claim for trade dispute 贸易纠纷（引起的）索赔
claim letter 索赔书
claim on 向某人（方）提出索赔
claim on the goods 对某（批）货索赔
claim report 索赔报告
claiming administration 索赔局
claims assessor 估损人
claims department/commission 索赔委员会
claims documents 索赔证件
claims rejected 拒赔
claims settlement 理赔
claims settling agent 理赔代理人
claims settling fee 理赔代理费
claims statement 索赔清单
claims surveying agent 理赔检验代理人
clause by clause 一条一条
closer inspection 严格检验
closing price 收盘价
coincide with 与……一致

collective packing 组合包装
come into effect 生效
commercial counselor 商务参赞
commercial invoice 商业发票
commodity futures 商品期货
completion of contract 完成合同
concerned parties 相关方
confirm an order 确认订单
congested market 横向市场盘整
consignment order 寄售单
construction spending 建筑支出
consumer pack/packing 零售包装，消费包装
continuous sampling 连续抽样
contract for future delivery 期货合同
contract for goods 订货合同
contract for purchase 采购合同
contract for service 劳务合同
contract law 合同法
contract life 合同有效期
contract note 买卖合同（证书）
contract of arbitration 仲裁合同
contract of carriage 运输合同
contract of employment 雇佣合同
contract of engagement 雇佣合同
contract of insurance 保险合同
contract of sale 销售合同
contract parties 合同当事人
contract period/contract term 合同期限
contract price 合同价格
contract provisions/stipulations 合同规定
contract sales 订约销售
contract terms/contract clauses 合同条款
contract wages 合同工资

Appendix A Glossary

contractual claim 按合同索偿
contractual damage 合同引起的损害
contractual dispute 合同上的争议
contractual guarantee 合同规定的担保
contractual income 合同收入
contractual joint venture 合作经营企业，契约式联合经营企业
contractual liability/obligation 合同规定的义务
contractual practice/usage 合同惯例
contractual specifications 合同规定
contractual terms & conditions 合同条款和条件
copies of the contract 合同副本
corrugated cardboard boxes 瓦楞纸纸箱
cost level 成本费用水平
cost of transportation 运输费
cost price 成本价
countersign a contract 会签合同
currency value goes way down 币值顿时跌落
current price 时价，现价
customary packing 习惯包装，惯用包装
daily chart 日图
Danish krone 丹麦克朗
date of delivery 交货日期
day trader 当日交易者
deal in 经营
declaration date 期权合约宣布的最后日期
delay shipment 延误装运
deliver goods 发货
delivery in installments 分批装运
delivery instructions 交货说明
delivery note 交货通知
delivery release 发货通知
delivery schedule 交货计划表
Deutsch mark 德国马克
direct shipment 直接装运
direct steamer (vessel) 直达船
dispatch advice 发运通知
dispatch goods 发货
dispatch money 速遣费
dispatch order 发运单
documentary credit 信用证
draft a contract 起草合同
draw up 起草
draw up a contract 拟定合同
drawn clause 出票条款
durable goods orders 耐用消费品订单
eat into our profits 耗掉了我们的利润
effect shipment 完成装运
European main ports (EMP) 欧洲主要口岸
employment report 就业报告
empty container bill 空集装箱提单
en route 在途中
enquiry list 询价单
enter into a contract 订合同
entry-exit inspection and quarantine bureau 进出口检验检疫局
entry-exit inspection and quarantine institution 进出口检验检疫机构
equivalent to 等于，折合
estimated time of arrival (ETA) 预抵期
estimated time of departure (ETD) 预离期
exceptional price 特价
exchange control declaration 结汇核销单
execute an order 执行订单
execute/implement/fulfil/perform a contract 执行合同

execution of contract　履行合同
executory contract　尚待执行的合同
exercise notice　期权履约通知
exercise price　期权履约价格
expiration of contract　合同期满
expiry date　到期日
export license application　出口许可证申请表
express shipment　快速装运
extra price　附加价
Food and Drug Administration (FDA)　（美国）食品及药物管理局
file a (one's) claim　提出索赔
final and binding　最后的依据并具有约束力
final and binding　最终并有约束力的
finalize the price　敲定价格
financial futures　金融期货
firm order　不可撤销的订单
first notice day　第一通知日
floor broker　场内经纪人
floor price　最低价
floor trader　证券交易所内的交易商
fluctuation　波动，涨落，起伏
follow the award　执行决议
for the buyer's account　由买方负担费用
force majeure　不可抗力
foreign exchange futures　外汇期货
forward exchange rate　远期汇率
forward market　远期市场
forward months　合约月份
free convertible currencies　可自由兑换通货（货币）
freight charge　运费
freight collect　运费到付

freight prepaid　运费预付
French franc　法国法郎
fresh option plays　新的期权买家
fresh order　新订单
fulfill an order　履行订单
get a contract　得到合同
get to the point　进入正题
go (enter) into force　生效
go over　浏览
go up in smoke　化为乌有
going price　现价
gross domestic product　国内生产总值
gross price　毛价
gross weight　总重，毛重
handle with care　小心轻放
hanging packing　挂式包装
hasten shipment　加快装运
have a bearing on　与……有关，对……有影响
hire order　租用单
hit and bit　拍板成交
Hong Kong dollar　港元
honor a contract　重合同，守约
immediate delivery　立刻交货
in charge of　负责
in compatible with　与……相容
in conformity with　和……相适应，和……一致（符合），遵照
in settlement of　解决
in stock　有存货
in terms of　在……方面
in the amount of　金额为……
inception of carriage　货车检查
incur some loss　造成损失
inspect A for B　检查A中是否有B

Appendix A Glossary

inspection after construction 施工后检验
inspection and acceptance 验收
inspection and certificate fee 检验签证费
inspection before delivery 交货前检验
inspection between process 工序间检验
inspection certificate 检验证明
inspection certificate of health 健康检验证书
inspection certificate of origin 产地检验证书
inspection certificate of quality 质量检验证书
inspection certificate of quantity 数量检验证书
inspection certificate of value 价值检验证书
inspection certificate of weight 重量检验证书
inspection certificate on damaged cargo 验残检验证书
inspection certificate on tank 验船证书
inspection during construction 在建工程检验
inspection of commodity 商品检验
inspection of document 单证检查
inspection of fixed asset 固定资产检查
inspection of incoming merchandise 到货验收
inspection of loading 监装检验
inspection of material 材料检验
inspection of packing 包装检验
inspection of risk 被保险物价的检查
inspection of storage 监装
inspection of voucher 凭证检验
inspection on cleanliness of dry cargo hold 干货舱清洁检验
inspection on cleanliness of tank 油舱清洁检验
inspection report 检验报告
inspection tag 检查标签
inspector of tax 税务稽查员
inspectorate general of customs 海关稽查总局
insurance certificate 保险凭证
insurance claim 保险索赔
insurance declaration sheet/bordereau 保险申报单/明细表
insurance policy 保险单
insurer's invoice 保险人发票
interpretation of contract 合同的解释
intraday 日内的，当天的
inverted market 倒挂市场
invoice number 发票号
invoicing data sheet 产品售价单
issue a certificate 出具证明
Italian lira 意大利里拉
Japanese yen 日元
job site 现场
keep away from boilers 远离锅炉
keep away from cold 请勿受冷
keep away from heat 请勿受热
keep dry 保持干燥
keep in a cool place 在冷处保管
land a contract 得到（拥有）合同
large stops 巨大的止损盘
last notice day 最后通知日
last trading day 最后交易日
lay days 受载日期，装卸时间
lead time 时间间隔
Let's call it a deal. （口）这笔交易就敲定

143

（拍板）吧。
letter of credit (L/C) （银行发行的）信用证
life of contract 合同期限
limit price 价格波动幅度限制
liquid market 买卖易于成交的市场，高流通性市场
lock in 锁定收益
lodge a (one's) claim 提出索赔
long distance delivery 长距离运输
long hedge 多头套期保值
long-term contract 长期合同
look forward to 盼望
look into 调查（查找）
lose out 输掉，亏本
make a (one's) claim 提出索赔
make a claim for (on) sth. 就某事提出索赔
make a claim with (against) sb. 向某人（方）提出索赔
make a contract 签订合同
make a reduction 减价
make an investigation 调查研究
make up 补偿
market maker 做市商
market participant 市场参与者
market price 市价
mate's receipt 大副收据
maximum price 最高价
maximum/minimum price 最大/最小价格波动
melt away 逐渐消失
minimum price 最低价
mode of transportation 运输方式
moderate price 公平价格
net price 净价
net weight 净重

new price 新价
nice fat contract 很有利的合同
no doubt 无疑
nominal price 名义价格，有价无市的价格（虚价）
non-negotiable B/L 不可转让提单
Norwegian krone 挪威克朗
notice day 通知日
official price 正式价格
old price 旧价
omnibus account 综合账户
on deck B/L 舱面提单
on the basis of 基于
on the grounds of... 因为……，由于……
on the high side （价格）偏高
on the small side 较小
one cancels other (OCO) 非此即彼订单
open contracts 未平仓合约
open order 开口订单
open outcry 公开喊价
opening price 开市价，开盘价
opening range 开市价幅
open-package inspection 开箱检验
open-package inspection 开箱检验
optional port 任意港
options committee 期权委员会
order B/L 指示提单
order form 订货单
original bill of lading 正本提单
original price 原价
originals of contract 合同正本
out-of-the-money option 虚值期权
outright forward exchange rate 直接远期汇率

词汇表 Appendix A Glossary

packing and presentation 包装及外观
packing charge/expense 包装费用
packing clause 包装条款
packing cost 包装成本
packing credit 打包放款，包装信用证
packing extra 包装费用另计
packing instruction 包装说明
packing list 装箱单
partial shipment 分批装运
pass on to 传递给……
performance of contract 合同的履行
place a contract 订合同
place an order with 向……订购
place our goods on the market (push the sale of our goods) 销售商品
port of destination 目的港
port of loading 装货港
port of shipment 装运港
port of unloading/discharge 卸货港
post receipt 邮政收据
pound sterling 英镑
predetermined rate 预定的汇率
present price 现价
prevailing price 现价
prevent sb. from doing sth. 阻止某人做某事
price calculation 价格计算
price card 价格目录
price catalogue 定价目录
price contract 价格合约
price control 价格控制
price current 市价表
price effect 价格效应
price format 价格目录，价格表
price index/price indices 价格指数
price limit 价格限制
price list 价格目录，价格单
price of commodities 物价
price of factory 厂价
price per unit 单价
price ratio 比价
price regulation 价格调整
price structure 价格构成
price support 价格支持
price tag 价格标签，标价条
price terms 价格条款
price theory 价格理论
price/sales catalogue 价格/销售目录
pricing cost 定价成本
pricing method 定价方法
pricing policy 定价政策
primary market 初级市场
prior to 在……以前
producer price index 生产者价格指数
product performance report 产品性能报告
product specification report 产品规格报告
production schedule 生产进度表
profit taking 获利回吐
promissory note 本票
prompt date 交割日期
prompt shipment 即期装运
punctual delivery 按期交货
purchase order 订购单
put in a (one's) claim 提出索赔
put option 看跌期权，延卖期权，卖出期权

quotations committee　报价委员会
raise a (one's) claim　提出索赔
reasonable fee　合理的费用
red tape　烦琐的官方手续
register a (one's) claim　提出索赔
registered representative　登记代表
regular liner　班机，班船
remittance advice　汇款通知
renewal of contract　合同的续订
repeat a contract　重复合同
repeat order　续订订单
resistance barrier　阻力价位
retail price　零售价
ring committee　场内交易委员会
ring dealing broker　交易会员
rising lows　低点上升
risk aversion　风险转移
round from oversold territory　离开超卖区域
ruling price　目前的价格
sales confirmation（S/C）　销售确认书
sale down　递跌买入
sales confirmation　销售确认书
sample order　样品订单
sanitary inspection certificate　卫生检验证书
sanitary standards　卫生标准
sea waybill　海运单
security deposit　保证金
see eye to eye (with somebody)　与（某人）意见一致
sell into strength strategy　逢高卖出
selling hedge　卖出套期保值
selling price　卖价

settle a claim　解决索赔（问题）
settlement business day　结算营业日
settlement price　结算价格
shipped B/L (on board B/L, shipped on board B/L)　装船提单
shipped quality, quantity, and weight　装货质量、数量和重量
shipper's letter of instructions (air)　托运人说明书（空运）
shipping advice　装船通知
shipping agent　装运代理商
shipping company　运输公司
shipping documents　装运单据
shipping instructions　装船指示，装运说明
shipping mark　唛头
short hedge　卖出套期保值
short sale　卖空
short selling　卖空
short squeeze　轧空头，逼空
short weight　重量不足
short-term contract　短期合同
sign a contract　签合同
Singapore dollar　新加坡元
so far　迄今为止
special price　特价
special risk　特种险
specific circumstance　特殊情况
spot market　现货市场
spot month　现货月
stale B/L　过期提单
stick to　坚持
stop-loss order　止损指令
stores requisition　领料单，库存物资请

Appendix A Glossary

领单
straight B/L 记名提单
strike price 成交价
strong market 坚挺的市场
submit dispute 提交争议申请
submit for arbitration 提交仲裁
support point 支持价位
swap order 换货单
Swedish krona 瑞典克朗
Swiss franc 瑞士法郎
take up 拿起，抱起
tanker bill of lading 油轮提单
tear up the contract 撕毁合同
terminate the contract 解除合同
terms of payment 付款条件
test lower 测试更低价位
test report 测试报告
The chances are… (probably) 可能是……
the commodities fair 商品交易会
the exact deadline of the loading period 确切的装船期限
the fixed-weight deflators 加权固定价格指数
the foreign trade contract 对外贸易合同
the implicit deflators 隐含价格指数
the last thing we want to do 我们最不想做的事是……
the season for this commodity 这个商品的销售季节
thin market 成交清淡的市场
through B/L 联运提单
tight market 成交活跃的市场
time limit 期限
time of shipment 装运期

time value 时间价值
timely shipment 及时装运
to effect shipment (= to make shipment) 装运（effect 意为"实现"）
to play safe 注意安全，稳重行事
to step up production 加快生产
to stow away with… 和……放在一起，与……收存在一起
to take… into account (consideration) 考虑，把……考虑进去
top quality 质量好
theft, pilferage and non-delivery (TPND) 偷窃提货不着险
tradable amount 市场允许的最小交易量
trade house 经纪行
trade house 贸易行
transshipment B/L 转船提单
trial order 试销订单
two-way market 双向市场
unclean B/L (dirty B/L, foul B/L) 不清洁提单
underlying futures contract 期权期货合约
unit of trading 交易单位
unit price 单价
Unites States dollar 美元
unofficial price 非正式价格
valid term 有效期
value spot 现汇价
variation margin 价格变动保证金
veterinary inspection certificate 动物检疫证明书
via Hong Kong 途经香港
volatile market 多变市场

147

waive a claim　放弃索赔（要求）
weak market　疲软的市场
weight certificate　重量证书
weight list　重量单
wholesale price　批发价
withdraw a claim　撤销（某项）索赔
written contract　书面合同
You cannot count on that.　你不要指望那个。
You may take it from me...　我可以向你保证……

References
参 考 文 献

[1] 陈祥国. 国际商务英语报刊选读[M]. 北京：中国商务出版社，2006.
[2] 顾乾毅. 国际商贸英语[M]. 广州：华南理工大学出版社，2005.
[3] 郭义伟. 实用商贸英语[M]. 北京：机械工业出版社，2004.
[4] 浩瀚. 金融服务英语急用句[M]. 北京：机械工业出版社，2007.
[5] 贺雪娟. 商务英语[M]. 北京：外语教学与研究出版社，2007.
[6] 黄芳. 国际商务英语[M]. 北京：中国商务出版社，2004.
[7] 贾建华，孙莹. 国际商务教程[M]. 北京：首都经济贸易大学出版社，2006.
[8] 李小飞，祝凤英. 商务英语阅读[M]. 北京：外语教学与研究出版社，2005.
[9] 廖瑛. 实用外贸谈判英语[M]. 北京：对外经济贸易大学出版社，2004.
[10] 廖瑛. 新编外贸英语口语教程[M]. 北京：对外经济贸易大学出版社，2006.
[11] 凌双英，王俊. 实用经贸英语口语[M]. 北京：高等教育出版社，2006.
[12] 刘白玉，高新华. 商务英语[M]. 苏州：苏州大学出版社，2009.
[13] 马德高. 商务交际高手[M]. 北京：世图音像电子出版社，2007.
[14] 盛小利. 商务英语谈判口语[M]. 北京：中国宇航出版社，2007.
[15] 王学成，齐欣. 国际商务英语[M]. 北京：中国金融出版社，2004.
[16] 张翠萍. 商贸英语口语大全[M]. 北京：对外经济贸易大学出版社，2006.
[17] 张丽敏，陈琛. 商务谈判英语[M]. 天津：天津科技翻译出版公司，2006.
[18] 张立玉. 商务谈判英语[M]. 武汉：武汉大学出版社，2009.
[19] 张志辉. 金融保险英语口语[M]. 北京：国防工业出版社，2004.
[20] 赵颖. 商务英语口语[M]. 北京：清华大学出版社，2007.
[21] 朱慧萍. 国际贸易英语谈判[M]. 上海：上海科学技术出版社，2006.
[22] 朱佩芬. 商务英语口语教程[M]. 北京：中国商务出版社，2004.